COWBOY

POETRY

COOKBOOK

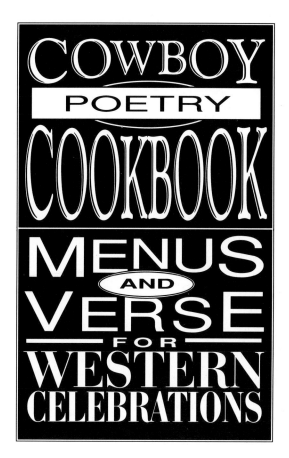

COWBOY POETRY COOKBOOK

MENUS AND VERSE FOR WESTERN CELEBRATIONS

CYD MCMULLEN
AND
ANNE WALLACE MCMULLEN

GIBBS·SMITH PUBLISHER

PEREGRINE SMITH BOOKS

SALT LAKE CITY

To our mothers and grandmothers,
whose ranch recipes and
wood stove cooking secrets
we inherited.

First edition

95 94 93 92   10 9 8 7 6 5 4 3 2 1

Color illustrations, menus, and introductions
copyright © 1992 by Gibbs Smith, Publisher

This is a Peregrine Smith Book,
published by
Gibbs Smith, Publisher
P.O. Box 667
Layton, UT 84041

Design by J. Scott Knudsen
Color illustrations by Carie Henrie
Line Illustrations by Katherine Fields and Fred Lambert
Manufactured in Singapore

Library of Congress Cataloging-in-Publication Data
McMullen, Cydnee R., 1949-
   Cowboy poetry cookbook: menus and verse for western
  celebrations / Cydnee R. McMullen & Anne Wallace McMullen.
     p. cm.
  Includes index
  ISBN 0-87905-457-3 (pbk.)
   1. Cookery, American–Western style. 2. West (U.S.) – Folklore.
3. American poetry – West (U.S.) I. McMullen, Anne Wallace, 1954- .
  II. Title.
TX715.2.W47M38 1992
641.5978–dc20   91-38690
                              CIP

CONTENTS

ACKNOWLEDGEMENTS

This cookbook was the brainchild of Gibbs Smith, Publisher. We thank them for inviting our participation.

Many cowboy poets and ranch cooks shared their poems and recipes with us. We truly appreciate their interest: Loo Burroughs, Denair, CA; Rolf Flake, Gilbert, AZ; June Brander Gilman, Drummond, MT; Art & Marianne Glaser, Halleck, NV; Charlie Hunt, Rapid City, SD; Della Johns, Elko, NV; Doug McCutcheon, Vinton, CA; Mary McMullen, Reno, NV; Sunny Martin, Ely, NV; Howard L. Norskog, St. Anthony, ID; Glenn Ohrlin, Mt. View, AK; Betty Ramsey, Amarillo, TX; Scott Redington, Big Horn, WY; Claudia Riordan, Jiggs, NV; Marie W. Smith, Somers, MT; and Charlotte Thompson, Round Mountain, NV.

We also thank our friends who tested recipes, contributed some of their own, made suggestions and offered encouragement when the task seemed an impossible one: Jeanette Baker, Thad Ballard, Meg Birak, Valerie Easterly, Genie Goicoechea, Jane Guisti, Mary McMullen, Richard McNally, Rod McQueary, Karen and Larry Martin, Katherine Ouellette, Nancy Remington, Sharon Thompson and Mary Walker.

We are indebted to Madge Baird for her editorial expertise and invaluable assistance in shaping the book.

Most of all we thank our family—Russ, Emily and Elena McMullen—for their patience, for sampling innumerable dishes in several different versions, and for making space in their lives for our project.

Katherine Field .35.

INTRODUCTION

Somewhere in the West tonight, cowboys sit around a campfire, gulping strong coffee from tin mugs, joshing each other about a missed toss or laughing again at an old yarn. At the edge of the firelight, old Cookie sets the sourdough for morning biscuits. Beyond the chuckwagon move the shadowy shapes of horses, the cavvy* restless, grazing under the moon.

At dawn, the scene changes as the eastern sky brightens to gray above the pine hills. In the kitchen, bright under electric lights, a woman leans over a wood stove, tending a skillet of sizzling bacon and a griddle of hotcakes turning gold. Sleepy-eyed children clump through the kitchen on their way to the barn and feeding chores, aromas of coffee and bacon and sweet maple syrup tantalizing empty stomachs.

The story of the cowboy, the rancher, the trail drive, the line camp, the chuck wagon has not ended—although it has changed some with electricity, the pickup truck, and satellite dishes. Now cattle are hauled in semi-loads to market, rather than trailed the long dusty way by a band of cowboys. Ranchers sometimes rely on all-terrain vehicles to irrigate land or check fences, rather than going afoot or horseback as their fathers did.

In the same spirit of change, foods associated with the West have been updated. Bacon and beans, beefsteak and sourdough are partnered on ranch tables with fresh vegetables, seafoods, exotic spices and flavors from a dozen ethnic traditions. The result is a new brand of western cooking with the same heartiness, the same welcoming tradition of hospitality that has made ranch meals so memorable.

This book is intended to help you recreate this crossbred ranch cooking in your own kitchen or camp. Recipes originally cooked over open fires or in balky wood stoves have been adapted for the modern kitchen and the backyard grill. But in the kitchen or chuckwagon, on the campfire or grill, the rules are the same: use what is available; keep it simple and straightforward; share it with friends; let good food and good company create the setting.

Food is celebration in cowboy culture. Brandings, roundups, ropings, haying are as much excuses for social gatherings as they are for sharing the work. Ranch people celebrate not only the work completed, but the bond that comes from working as a team. More than the special foods that are made for these occasions, the key ingredient is the sense of welcome any stranger recognizes when he is invited to "sit down and eat a bite."

This gathering of recipes comes from many sources. Ranch cooks from several states opened their recipe boxes to us. Relatives dug up recipes of our ranching ancestors and helped us remember preparations passed down by word of mouth. Wood-stove specialists gave us advice, and one or two chuckwagon cooks came out of retirement to tell their stories.

With these menus and a group of congenial people, you can create a cowboy country celebration in your own setting. You might even pull on your boots, hat and bandana, sing an old-time cowboy song or two, and recite some classic cowboy poems!

*short for *caballada,* string of horses.

Katherine Field - 33

3 pounds steak or sliced ham
¼ cup water
¼ cup flour
2 cups milk
Salt
Pepper

4 potatoes
Water
1 tablespoon salt
Flour

WORKIN' HAND'S CHUCKWAGON BREAKFAST

"You are sleepin' in your hot roll when somebody
    kicks your tarp.
When you roll out of your blankets why the wind
    feels cold and sharp..."

(from "Second Guard" by Bruce Kiskaddon)

The buckaroo's day begins before the light. When he rolls out of his bedroll, he looks forward to a "stick-to-your-ribs" breakfast, for it may be his only meal until he rides back to the wagon at day's end.

The chuckwagon cook (variously called Cookie, Ol' Cooky, or Coosie) has rolled out even earlier to stoke up the fire, get a fresh pot of coffee on the coals, and stir up his sourdough. His ingredients are staples, and his tools aren't fancy: a Dutch oven, a cast-iron frying pan, an enamel coffee pot blackened by many campfires. If he knows his trade, his biscuits or hotcakes are light, his bacon is crisp, and his cowboys are happy.

STEAK OR HAM WITH COUNTRY GRAVY
Serves 6

In a large cast iron skillet fry steak or ham. Add water to the pan and stir to lift brown bits. Sprinkle in flour, stirring to prevent lumps. Add milk, a small amount at a time, stirring constantly until gravy reaches the proper consistency. Add salt and pepper to taste. Serve gravy over meat.

TRADITIONAL SOURDOUGH STARTER

Peel and quarter potatoes. In a large pot boil potatoes in plenty of water. When potatoes are soft, remove from pot, reserving the liquid. Cool potato water. Add salt and enough flour to make a thin batter. Pour batter into gallon-size earthenware crock. Cover with cheesecloth so that the batter can absorb wild yeast from the air.

BEDROLL
Red Steagall

There's a hole in the wagonsheet big as my head
Where coosie run under a tree.
Last week it rained and poured right in that hole;
Probably nobody noticed but me.

'Cause that was the mornin' I jingled the horses.
It rained and my bed was just fine.
But it was the first one to go in the wagon
And the rest of 'em stacked up on mine.

Last winter we put a new floor in that wagon,
We planked it with tongue and groove oak.
She's tight as a drum and won't leak a drop.
So the bed on the bottom got soaked.

Now canvas is good about turnin' the dew
As long as it's stretched the right way.
But I guess something happens, it sorta breaks down
Sittin' in water all day.

Your bed's usually warm and a nice place to be,
A cowpuncher's private domain.
But it's colder'n hell in a bedroll that's wet;
You're better off out in the rain.

So I put on my slicker and sat by the fire,
Burned all the dry wood in the stack.
The fire made me drowsy—once I dozed off
And woke up in the mud, on my back.

Just before sunup I crawled in that bed,
Couldn't sleep 'cause my feet were so numb.
Then coosie was cussin' I burned all his wood,
So I got up and gathered him some.

Now I ain't one to argue and create a fuss
And I don't get my head in a fog.
But it's taken a week for me to get her dried out,
And last night I slept like a log.

This mornin' it's thunderin' and carryin' on.
It's already startin' to rain.
And I know for a fact coosie ain't fixed that hole
And I ain't goin' through that again.

Everyone's saddled and ready to ride
Except me, and I'll be here awhile.
I wanta make sure that when they load up the wagon
My bed's on the top of the pile.

Keep in a warm place (behind the wood stove) for 2 or 3 days or until batter is sour.

To keep the starter active, add 1 cup of warm water and about 1 cup of flour after each use. Remember to use wooden utensils and crockery bowls or other non-reactive metal utensils and containers when working with sourdough. For best results, your sourdough should be replenished at least once a week.

½ package (1 ¼ teaspoons) active dry yeast
½ cup warm water
2 cups flour
2 cups water
2 tablespoons sugar

MODERN SOURDOUGH STARTER

Stir together yeast and ½ cup warm water. Let stand until yeast has dissolved. Combine flour, 2 cups water, and sugar in a gallon size earthenware crock. Add yeast mixture and beat well. Cover with cheesecloth and let stand in a warm place about 2 days. Never cover the crock tightly as the starter needs to breathe.

To keep the starter active, add one cup of warm water and about 1 cup of flour after each use. Remember to use wooden utensils and crockery bowls or other non-reactive metal utensils and containers when working with sourdough. For best results, your sourdough should be replenished at least once a week.

SOURDOUGH STARTERS

Starters become old friends, and with repeated use you will develop an idea of how to control the sourness to suit your own tastes. The addition of soda in your recipes will also affect the sourness of your finished product. If too much soda is used, the product will be brownish when baked. If too little soda is used, the product is too sour. Always add the soda just before baking and NEVER to the starter as it kills the yeast. It is best to reserve a bit of the liquid you are using to dissolve the soda before adding it.

If your starter should sit unused for 2 or 3 weeks, spoon out half of it and replenish with the warm water and flour. If you don't expect to use your starter for several weeks or more, place it in the freezer. This will slow down the action of the yeast. Before using, thaw starter and leave it at room temperature at least 24 hours.

3 cups flour, sifted
2 cups Sourdough Starter
1 tablespoon baking powder
1 teaspoon sugar
½ teaspoon salt

SOURDOUGH BISCUITS
Makes about 2 dozen

Place flour in a large bowl; make a hollow in its center. Pour starter into the hollow. Add baking powder, sugar, and salt. Mix into a soft dough. On a floured board roll out dough ½ inch thick and cut into rounds. Place dough in a large greased rectangular pan or in a Dutch oven. Brush tops of biscuits with butter and let stand for 10 minutes. Bake in a 500 degree oven for 10 minutes or till golden brown.

BUCKAROO COFFEE

My grandfather, Mark Scott, ran the IL Ranch in northern Elko County for several years. He spent his life in the cattle business; at various times he was a buckaroo, a rancher, a cattle buyer, and a brand inspector. He liked his coffee strong and hot, with a little Sego milk stirred in.

Poppop, as I called him, carried a large enamel coffee pot blackened by the soot of many campfires. He filled the pot with cold water, threw in 2 large handfuls of coffee, and set the pot on the fire to boil. When the brew began to smell like coffee, he dropped an egg into the pot to settle the grounds. He set that strong black coffee at the edge of his fire, ready for a passing cowboy or fisherman to share a cup and pass the time of day.

SOURDOUGH HOTCAKES
Serves 6

The night before making hotcakes, put the starter into large crockery mixing bowl. Stir in the flour and enough water to make a medium batter. Cover and let stand at room temperature overnight. (Remember to replenish your starter with 1 cup flour and 1 cup warm water.) In the morning, stir in beaten eggs, butter or oil, sugar, and baking soda. Let rise for a few minutes, then drop batter onto a hot griddle. Cook till golden brown, turning to cook both sides.

2 cups Sourdough Starter
1 cup flour
Water
2 beaten eggs
1 tablespoon sugar
2 tablespoons melted butter
  or cooking oil
1 tablespoon baking soda

POPPOP'S HOTCAKES
Serves 6

In a bowl stir together flour, sugar, baking powder, and salt. Add the cream and eggs. Add enough milk to thin batter to desired consistency. Spoon batter onto a hot griddle. Cook till golden brown, turning to cook both sides.

4 cups flour
¼ cup sugar
2 tablespoons plus 2
  teaspoons baking
  powder
½ teaspoon salt
1 to 2 cups light cream
2 beaten eggs
Milk

COMPANY BREAKFAST AT THE COOKHOUSE

At the home ranch, breakfast for company is still served at dawn, and latecomers are teased about "burning daylight." Guests and cowboys sit down together at long tables, load their plates with steaming heaps of eggs and ham, and slather baking powder biscuits with butter and jelly. The cook passes behind the benches keeping platters stocked and coffee mugs filled. Whether the day's work is weighing cattle and loading them into trucks for shipping, or driving to a rodeo for team roping in the next valley, everyone who eats at the cookhouse table is expected to eat a hearty breakfast. That goes for the rancher, his cowboy crew, the cattle buyer, and the city folks in brand new boots.

MENU

SCRAMBLED EGGS WITH CHORIZO

HOMEMADE SALSA

ROCKY BAR HASH BROWNS

ROASTED PEPPERS

MILE-HIGH BISCUITS

MAPLE PECAN MUFFINS

HONEY MUSTARD AND CHEESE MUFFINS

BRAN MUFFINS

CHOKECHERRY JELLY

4 to 5 chorizo sausages
12 large eggs, beaten
2 tablespoons butter or margarine

SCRAMBLED EGGS WITH CHORIZO
Serves 6

Chorizos are the spicy sausages familiar in the West wherever there are concentrations of Basque peoples. For authenticity, be sure to specify Basque chorizos when ordering from the meat market. Mexican varieties are somewhat hotter and spicier.

To prepare chorizos, arrange them on a rack which has been placed in a pan above one inch of water. Cover. Bake at 350 degrees for 1 hour. Slice or dice warm sausages. (This step may be done ahead.)

In a large skillet melt butter or margarine. Add eggs and cook over medium heat, stirring to scramble. Fold in sausages when the eggs have just begun to set. Serve with Homemade Salsa.

A WORKING RANCH
Gwen Petersen

"We envy you," said my city friends,
"Your life in the great outdoors.
We're thinking of buying a ranch somewhere
And living a life like yours.

"We'll have a garden—our very own,
and keep lots of animals there;
A working ranch," they said—and smiled,
And their eyes held a faraway stare.

In my ears I can hear their words ring plain
As I start on my morning chore;
With two heavy buckets of water and grain
I head for the chicken house door.

As I enter the scabby, unpainted shed
To a roomful of clucking hens,
I see the gazebo with white wicker chairs
On the lawn of my city friends.

I picture them tossing sunflower seeds
To a twittering songbird band.
Then a setting hen ends my reverie
By pecking a hole in my hand.

I leave with my bucket of fresh-laid eggs
And step in a juicy cowpie;
My feet do the splits—I crash in the dirt
And the eggs fly off for the sky.

As I lie supine, I spy from the ground
That the garden gate is awry,
And there six heifers are munching around
In my summer food supply.

My two frantic collies and I commence
To bark and scream and yell;
The heifers depart by way of the fence,
Trampling it all to—well.

I fix the fence and enter the house
As a neighbor phones to say
That my horses have wandered into his field
And are eating his prime cut hay.

And do I want my registered saddle mare bred
To his workhorse stud, asks he.
"No, no!" I screech, and filled with dread,
I move with alacrity.

My city friends wear designer jeans;
My city friends eat quiche;
They have a courtyard full of flowers
And poodles trained to the leash.

But they yearn for a working ranch, they claim,
To experience its joys and its fun.
Another day like this has been
And, hell—I'll give 'em this one.

Gwen Petersen is a ranch woman who writes and publishes several books of poetry. She lives in Big Timber MT.

1 28-ounce can crushed tomatoes
1 14-ounce can plum tomatoes,
  chopped, with juice
1 10-ounce can tomato paste
4 small firm tomatoes, chopped
½ cup chopped onion
¼ to ½ cup fresh cilantro, snipped
2 cloves garlic, crushed
3 to 7 fresh jalapeño peppers,
  finely chopped
1 to 2 tablespoons brown sugar
1 tablespoon ground coriander
Salt
¼ cup fresh lime juice (juice
  of 2 limes)
¼ to ½ cup tequila (optional)

HOMEMADE SALSA
Makes about 6 cups

In a large crockery bowl stir together crushed tomatoes, plum tomatoes, tomato paste, fresh tomatoes, onion, cilantro, and garlic. Taste for sweetness; if quite sweet, cut or eliminate brown sugar. Stir in jalapeños, brown sugar, and coriander. Add salt to taste. Cover and refrigerate for 30 minutes. Thin to desired consistency with lime juice and tequila. Store in jars and keep refrigerated. Keeps up to 1 week.

6 potatoes
1 medium onion, chopped
⅓ red bell pepper, chopped
Olive oil
Salt
Cajun-style seasoning

ROCKY BAR HASH BROWNS
Serves 6

Cowboy Poetry Gathering volunteer Larry Martin has become famous for these potatoes. Larry prefers to use tender new potatoes from his garden.

Grate the raw potatoes with the large side of the grater or the large grating disk of a food processor. Heat enough olive oil to cover the bottom of a large cast-iron skillet. Add the potatoes and cook the potatoes over medium heat, stirring to keep them from sticking together. When potatoes are half cooked, add onion and bell pepper. Season with salt and Cajun Seasoning. Cook without stirring, until potatoes are brown and crisp on the bottom. Turn and continue cooking until both sides are brown and crisp.

6 bell peppers (combination of
  red, yellow, orange, and green)
¼ cup olive oil
2 tablespoons balsamic vinegar
Salt
Pepper
Fresh basil

ROASTED PEPPERS
Serves 6 to 8

To remove skin from peppers, hold each pepper over a gas flame until skin is charred. Or, place all the peppers on a baking sheet under the broiler and turn until all sides are charred. Place charred peppers in a bowl and cover with a wet towel. After 15 minutes, remove skin from peppers. Remove stems and seeds and slice in strips. Stir together peppers, oil, and vinegar. Season with salt and pepper. Marinate at least 1 hour or overnight. Serve at room temperature. Garnish with basil.

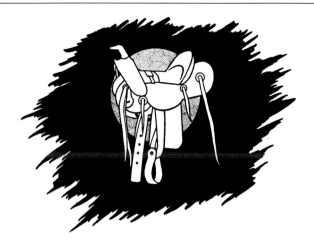

3 cups sifted flour
4 ½ teaspoons baking powder
2 ½ tablespoons sugar
¾ teaspoon cream of tartar
¾ teaspoon salt
¾ cup shortening
1 egg
1 cup milk

MILE-HIGH BISCUITS
Makes about 24 biscuits

Preheat oven to 450 degrees. Grease baking sheet. In a bowl sift flour, baking powder, sugar, cream of tartar, and salt. Cut in shortening with a pastry blender or two knives until mixture resembles coarse crumbs. Beat egg lightly and add to milk. Add milk mixture to flour mixture, stirring with fork until dough holds together. Turn dough onto floured board and knead 10 to 15 times. Do not knead too much. Roll dough out 1 inch thick and cut into biscuits with floured biscuit cutter. Arrange biscuits on baking sheet and bake in preheated oven for 12 minutes or till golden brown.

1 ¾ cups flour
2 ½ teaspoons baking powder
¼ teaspoon salt
1 cup pure maple syrup
¼ cup unsalted butter, melted
1 egg
¼ cup milk
½ cup chopped pecans

MAPLE PECAN MUFFINS
Makes about 12 muffins

In a large bowl stir together flour, baking powder, and salt. Combine syrup, melted butter, egg, and milk. Add syrup mixture and nuts all at once to flour mixture. Fold gently just till moistened. Grease or line muffin cups. Fill each cup ¾ full with batter. Bake in 400 degree oven about 15 minutes or until muffins are golden brown.

HONEY MUSTARD AND CHEESE MUFFINS
Makes about 12 muffins

In a large bowl stir together flour, baking powder, salt, and pepper. In another bowl use a wire whisk to mix the milk, cheese, egg, butter, mustard, and honey. Fold gently just till moistened. Grease or line muffin cups. Fill each cup ¾ full with batter. Bake in 400 degree oven about 15 minutes or until muffins are golden brown.

2 cups flour
1 tablespoon baking powder
¼ teaspoon salt
⅛ teaspoon fresh ground pepper
1 ¼ cups milk
1 cup grated cheddar cheese
1 egg
¼ cup melted butter
3 tablespoons honey mustard
2 tablespoons honey

BRAN MUFFINS
Makes about 24 muffins

Pour boiling water over 1 ½ cups of the bran flakes. Let stand. Meanwhile, in a large bowl stir together flour, brown sugar, baking soda, and salt. In another bowl combine buttermilk, oil, and eggs. Add bran mixture. Add to flour mixture. Fold gently just till moistened. Fold in raisins and nuts, if desired. Grease or line muffin cups. Fill each cup ¾ full with batter. Bake in 400 degree oven about 20 minutes or until muffins are golden brown. If desired, store batter in the refrigerator in a covered container for up to 6 weeks.

3 cups bran flakes or buds cereal
1 cup boiling water
2 ½ cups flour
1 ½ cups brown sugar
2 ½ teaspoons baking soda
1 teaspoon salt
2 cups buttermilk
1 cup vegetable oil
2 eggs, beaten
½ cup raisins (optional)
⅓ cup walnuts, chopped (optional)

CHOKECHERRY JELLY
Makes four 8-ounce jars

Chokecherries grow wild in canyons and high mountain passes in the west. In early summer the white blossoms lining mountain roads signal a good chokecherry harvest. Indians and white pioneers alike valued the fruit for its flavor—once sweetening was added! The bitter flavor of the raw berry gave it its name. Any local berries may be substituted for the chokecherries, but be sure to adjust the sugar and pectin as needed.

Rinse and drain chokecherries. Place in a 4-quart saucepan and add water just to cover berries. Bring to a boil over medium heat. Cover and reduce heat to low. Simmer until berries are very soft, stirring occasionally. Remove pan from heat; cool.

Place a dishtowel or several layers of cheesecloth in a colander or large strainer. Place the cooked berries in the cloth-lined sieve in batches, pressing gently to release the juice. Continue until you have five cups of juice. Discard the remaining pulp and pits. Add the sugar to the juice and bring to a boil, stirring constantly. Immediately stir in the pectin and boil for 1 minute or until the pectin is dissolved. Skim any foam from the surface. Ladle jelly into sterilized jars ½ inch from top. Cool slightly and seal with paraffin. When jars are completely cool, cover with lids.

2 quarts chokecherries
Water
6 cups sugar
1 package pectin

MENU

BLOODY MARY

ROCKY MOUNTAIN OYSTERS WITH SPECIAL SAUCE

BAKED HAM WITH SUPREME GLAZE

HAM STRATA

PARTY QUICHE

HASH BROWNS

THREE-HOUR ORANGE ROLLS

LEMON LOAF

ANNE'S CINNAMON ROLLS

BLUEBERRY COFFEECAKE

KIWI TART

COFFEE

1 ½ ounce vodka
¼ teaspoon Worcestershire sauce
Dash Tabasco sauce
6 ounces V-8 vegetable juice
Salt
Pepper
Lime wedge

ARTHUR GLASER'S COWBOY POETRY BRUNCH

Halleck, Nevada, is ranch country and the seat of Glaser Bros. Land and Livestock, where Art and Marianne Glaser annually host the Sunday brunch that winds up the Cowboy Poetry Gathering held in Elko in late January.

Driving east from Elko, you turn south on the Secret Pass road, cross the Humboldt River, and turn in at the gate of a long, low house set in a circle of trees. You are welcomed into a home crowded with poets, staff, supporters, ranch neighbors, and new friends made only days before at the Gathering.

Guests drop in over a four-hour period, and the buffet is constantly replenished. Neighbors help out by bringing their favorite sweet breads, coffee cakes or rolls. But the most celebrated dish of the meal is Art Glaser's special recipe of Rocky Mountain Oysters. Named to fool city folk with squeamish appetites, these are the testicles of young bull calves that have been turned into steers to increase weight gain and control the blood lines of beef-producing stock. The oysters have a delicate flavor and texture and are served with a piquant sauce.

BLOODY MARY
Makes 1 drink

In a large glass filled with ice combine vodka, Tabasco sauce, and Worcestershire sauce. Fill with V-8. Season to taste with salt and pepper. Squeeze the lime over the top.

THE BUNKHOUSE ORCHESTRA
Badger Clark

This poem can be sung to the tune of "Turkey in the Straw."

Wrangle up your mouth-harps, drag your banjo
   out,
Tune your old guitarra till she twangs right stout,
For the snow is on the mountains and the wind is
   on the plain,
But we'll cut the chimney's moanin' with a livelier
   refrain.

Shinin' 'dobe fireplace, shadows on the wall—
(See old Shorty's friv'lous toes a-twitchin' at the
   call:)
It's the best damn high that there is within the law
When seven jolly punchers tackle "Turkey in the
   Straw."

Freezy was the day's ride, lengthy was the trail,
Ev'ry steer was haughty with a high arched tail,
But we held 'em and we shoved 'em, for our
   longin' hearts were tried
By a yearnin' for tobacker and our dear fireside.

Swing 'er into stop-time, don't you let 'er droop!
(You're about as tuneful as a coyote with the
   croup!)
Ay, the cold wind bit when we drifted down the
   draw,
But we drifted on to comfort and to "Turkey in the
   Straw."

Snarlin' when the rain whipped, cussin' at the
   ford—
Ev'ry mile of twenty was a long discord,
But the night is brimmin' music and its glory is
   complete
When the eye is razzle-dazzled by the flip o' Shorty's
   feet!

Snappy for the dance, now till she up and shoots!
(Don't he beat the devil's wife for jiggin' in 'is
   boots?)
Shorty got throwed high and we laughed till he was
   raw,
But tonight he's done forgot it prancin' "Turkey in
   the Straw."

Rainy dark or firelight, bacon rind or pie,
Livin' is a luxury that don't come high;
Oh, be happy and unruly while our years and luck
   allow,
For we all must die or marry less than forty years
   from now!

Lively on the last turn! Lope 'er to the death!
(Reddy's soul is willin' but he's gettin' short o'
   breath.)
Ay, the storm wind sings and old trouble sucks his
   paw
When we have an hour of firelight set to "Turkey in
   the Straw."

4 pounds mountain oysters
½ cup flour
Salt
Pepper
½ teaspoon garlic powder (optional)
Cooking oil

ROCKY MOUNTAIN OYSTERS WITH SPECIAL SAUCE
Serves 12

Mountain oysters (sometimes called prairie oysters) can be ordered from your local butcher. Be sure to place your order well in advance. Serve these alongside a large skillet of scrambled eggs.

Place flour in a bowl. Add salt and pepper to taste. Stir in garlic powder, if desired. To clean oysters, peel off skin sacs by cutting a slash in them and squeezing until the egg-shaped oysters pop out. Roll them in flour mixture. Fry in hot oil over medium high heat until well done and crisp. Serve with Special Sauce.

2 cups chili sauce
½ cup prepared horseradish
½ teaspoon Tabasco sauce
⅓ cup lemon juice
½ cup finely chopped green pepper
½ cup finely chopped red pepper
½ cup finely chopped onion

SPECIAL SAUCE
Makes about 4 cups

In a bowl stir together chili sauce, horseradish, lemon juice, and Tabasco sauce. Add green pepper, red pepper, and onion. Stir till well combined. Cover and chill till serving time.

2 cups packed brown sugar
½ cup butter or margarine, softened
2 teaspoons ground cinnamon
½ teaspoon ground nutmeg
½ teaspoon ground cloves
Rind of 1 lemon, grated

SUPREME GLAZE FOR BAKED HAM

In a bowl stir together brown sugar, butter, cinnamon, nutmeg, cloves, and lemon peel. Store in the refrigerator. Spread over ham during the last 30 minutes of baking.

HAM STRATA
Serves 12

Line a 13x9-inch baking dish with half of the bread. Combine ham, celery, onion, and mushrooms; spread over bread layer. Add second bread layer. Stir together eggs, milk, and mayonnaise; pour over second bread layer. Cover and refrigerate overnight. Before baking, spoon on soup and sprinkle with cheese. Bake at 325 degrees for 1 hour.

10 slices white bread, buttered
1 cup cubed ham
1 cup diced celery
1 small onion, finely chopped
1 4-ounce can mushroom slices, drained
4 eggs, beaten
1 cup mayonnaise
2 cups milk
1 can condensed cream of mushroom soup
2 tablespoons grated cheddar cheese

PARTY QUICHE
Serves 15

Roll pie crust into a 20x15-inch rectangle; place in a 13x9-inch baking pan. Cover with plastic wrap and refrigerate at least 30 minutes. Remove crust from refrigerator and rub with softened butter. Fry bacon until crisp; drain and crumble. Sprinkle bacon and cheese over crust. Heat oven to 400 degrees. Stir together eggs, cream, salt, black pepper, cayenne pepper, nutmeg, and sugar. Pour over bacon and cheese. Bake for 15 minutes. Reduce heat to 300 degrees and bake another 30 minutes. Let stand 15 minutes before serving.

Piecrust for a 2-crust pie
1 tablespoon butter or margarine, softened
1 pound sliced bacon
½ pound Swiss cheese, grated
8 eggs, beaten
4 cups light cream
1 ½ teaspoons salt
Dash black pepper
Dash cayenne pepper
Dash nutmeg
Dash sugar

THREE-HOUR ORANGE ROLLS
Makes 24 rolls

Dissolve yeast in ¼ cup warm water. In a large bowl combine sugar, shortening, and salt. Stir in 1 cup warm water; cool. Add eggs and flour. Stir well. Let rise until double in bulk. Cover and refrigerate at least 2 hours or overnight. Remove from the refrigerator 3 hours before serving.

Roll dough into a ½ inch thick rectangle. Stir together sugar, butter or margarine, and orange rind; spread over dough. Using your hands, roll dough lengthwise and slice into 2- or 3-inch rolls. Place each roll in the cup of a greased muffin tin. Let rise for 3 hours at room temperature. Bake at 350 degrees for 15 minutes.

2 packages (5 teaspoons) active dry yeast
¼ cup warm water
½ cup sugar
½ cup shortening
2 teaspoons salt
1 cup warm water
3 eggs, beaten
4 ½ cups flour
Rind of 1 orange, grated
½ cup sugar
⅓ cup melted butter or margarine

½ cup butter or margarine
1 cup sugar
3 tablespoons lemon juice
4 eggs
4 cups flour, sifted
1 tablespoon baking powder
2 teaspoons salt
1 ½ cups milk
1 ½ cups coarsely chopped walnuts
Rind of 1 lemon, grated
4 teaspoons lemon juice
⅔ cup sifted powdered sugar

LEMON LOAF
Makes 1 loaf

Preheat oven to 350 degrees. In large bowl beat butter or margarine with an electric mixer at medium speed until light and fluffy. Slowly add sugar and beat on low speed till well combined. Beat in 3 tablespoons lemon juice. Add eggs, one at a time, beating well after each addition. Stir together flour, baking powder, and salt. Add to egg mixture alternately with milk, beating well after each addition. Fold in nuts and lemon peel. Pour into 1 greased 9x5-inch loaf pan or 2 greased 7x3-inch loaf pans. Bake 1 hour and 25 minutes for large loaf and 1 hour for small loaves or until toothpick inserted in loaf comes out clean. Let stand for 10 minutes; then loosen and remove from pans. Cool.

For glaze, stir together powdered sugar and 4 teaspoons lemon juice till smooth. Spread over top of bread. Wrap in plastic wrap and store at room temperature until ready to serve.

1 ½ cups scalded milk
1 cup butter
6 tablespoons sugar
2 teaspoons salt
1 package active dry yeast
¼ cup warm water
2 eggs, well beaten
6 cups flour
3 cups packed dark brown sugar
1 cup butter, melted
Ground cinnamon

ANNE'S CINNAMON ROLLS
Makes 48 rolls

These rolls can be made ahead and frozen. To serve, wrap them well in foil and place in the oven for 20 minutes or until thawed and warmed through. Place the rolls in a basket and serve immediately.

Combine the scalded milk with the butter, sugar, and salt. Dissolve the yeast in the warm water. When the milk mixture has cooled, add the yeast mixture and eggs. Stir in the flour, 1 cup at a time, till well combined. Transfer to a floured board and knead well until the dough is smooth and elastic. This will take at least 10 minutes. Place the dough in a well greased bowl and cover. Let rise in a warm place for 1 ½ to 2 hours or till doubled. Punch the dough down and allow to rise again for 1 ½ hours.

Separate the dough into 4 equal portions. Flatten 1 portion and shape into a large rectangle. Spread with ¾ cup of the brown sugar and ¼ cup of the melted butter. Sprinkle liberally and evenly with ground cinnamon. Roll and slice into 2-inch rolls. Place the rolls in a greased 13x9-inch baking pan. Dot the top of each roll with a small piece of butter and cover with a soft cloth. Allow to rise 15 minutes before baking. Repeat the procedure with the remaining dough. Bake at 375 degrees for 12 to 15 minutes. Remove the pan from the oven. Turn the rolls onto a cooling rack.

KIWI TART
Serves 8

For crust, pat cookie dough into a quiche pan and bake as directed. Cool.

In a bowl beat cream cheese, powdered sugar, and vanilla till smooth. Spread over cooled crust. Top in circular pattern with mandarin oranges, kiwi fruit, and bananas.

In a saucepan stir together sugar and cornstarch. Stir in orange juice, water, and lemon juice. Cook and stir till thickened and bubbly. Cook and stir 2 minutes more. Cool slightly. Spoon over fruit. Chill thoroughly before serving.

1 package refrigerated sugar cookie dough
1 8-ounce package cream cheese
1 cup sifted powdered sugar
1 teaspoon vanilla
Mandarin orange sections
Sliced kiwi fruit
Sliced bananas
¾ cup sugar
3 tablespoons cornstarch
1 cup orange juice
¾ cup water
¼ cup lemon juice

BLUEBERRY COFFEE CAKE
Serves 9

This good basic coffee cake recipe works equally well with apples, peaches, or other seasonal berries.

Combine brown sugar, 2 tablespoons flour, 2 tablespoons butter or margarine, and cinnamon. Set aside. In a bowl beat ¼ cup butter or margarine till softened. Beat in sugar. Gradually beat in egg and milk. Add flour, baking powder and salt, beating till well combined.

Pour half of the batter into a greased 9x9-inch baking dish. Layer with half of the blueberries. Sprinkle with half of the brown sugar mixture. Top with remaining batter, berries, and brown sugar mixture. Bake at 350 degrees for 50 to 60 minutes or until cake is set and golden brown.

½ cup packed brown sugar
2 tablespoons flour
2 tablespoons butter or margarine
2 teaspoons ground cinnamon
¼ cup butter or margarine
¾ cup sugar
1 egg
½ cup milk
1 ½ cups flour, sifted
2 teaspoons baking powder
½ teaspoon salt
3 cups fresh or frozen blueberries

Biscuits or thick bread slices
Marinated Chuck Roast
Coarse mustard
Roasted turkey
Sliced red onion

SADDLEBAG LUNCH

Lunch is a word cowboys don't like to use. It's part of the cowboy code that a sturdy man can fill up on breakfast and go all day until supper. Especially when working cattle on the range, stopping for lunch is impossible, because the cattle won't wait while you eat. But if the cowboys are working near enough to the cookhouse, they come in for a noon meal (called dinner), often the heartiest meal of the day. Or they may have their noon meal served from the modern-day chuckwagon—the bed of a pickup truck.

The biscuit sandwiches below are the traditional version. Leftover morning biscuits filled with bacon often found their way into a cowboy's pocket. Here we have included other western hunger-stoppers like jerky and dried fruit. They are a cowboy's "fast food"—easy to pack, quick to eat—even in the saddle with one hand on the reins.

Try packing a lunch like this for your next trail ride, be it on horse, bike, or in a two-door Bronco.

BISCUIT SANDWICHES

On a cattle drive or trail ride, compact sandwiches make the ideal lunch. Sourdough biscuits left from breakfast filled with meats left over from supper the night before were wrapped up to tuck in a pocket or saddlebag. For variety, use roasted turkey slices and a milder mustard, slices of sweet red onion, and sharp cheddar cheese. Or try these fillers in a variety of combinations: hard-cooked eggs, sweet pickles, watercress, thin-sliced celery, chopped green onions and crumbled bacon.

Just fill your biscuits or thick bread slices with the sliced beef and a strong coarse mustard and you are ready for the day.

Rolf M. Flake

When I was a kid, we always ate
    Breakfast, dinner, and then supper.
And "lunch" was somethin' you put in a sack,
    Or in a container named "Tupper."

We ate pretty good—three squares a day.
    Breakfast was always a treat—
With dinner at noon, supper at night.
    For at least two of those meals we ate meat.

Sometimes we'd miss dinner—just eat a lunch
    (Like I say, it was out of a sack),
But breakfast was sure, supper was too—
    Of good eatin' there was never a lack.

So I kinda feel sorry for people today
    Who eat breakfast, "lunch," and then dinner
And go to bed without SUPPER. I shouldn't worry, I guess—
    'Cause they sure don't appear any thinner.

MARINATED CHUCK ROAST

Marinating meat is a recent approach to using the less tender cuts of meat that were traditionally used for stews or other slow-cooked meals. By marinating a chuck steak overnight, you can grill it to a medium-rare stage without worrying that your guests will need a hacksaw to cut it.

    Combine all the ingredients except the meat in a deep glass dish. Mix well. Add the meat, turning to coat. Allow the meat to marinate in the refrigerator overnight. To cook, grill the meat over a slow fire. Allow it to cook approximately 30 minutes on each side (less for rarer meat). If the meat appears to dry out during cooking, baste with the marinade. Remove the roast to a serving dish and thin-slice it on the diagonal.

1 cup soy sauce
¼ cup brown sugar
2 tablespoons fresh ginger
    root, grated
2 tablespoons sesame oil
2 tablespoons vegetable oil
4 cloves garlic, pressed
¼ teaspoon black pepper
4 pounds chuck roast,
    approximately three inches
    thick

3 pounds lean venison
1 tablespoon salt
1 teaspoon onion powder
1 teaspoon garlic powder
1 to 2 teaspoons pepper
⅓ cup Worcestershire sauce
¼ cup soy sauce
1 tablespoon prepared mustard

DEER HUNTER'S JERKY
Approximately 30 to 40 strips

Jerky, the dried spiced meat strips which were probably adopted from the Native Americans, has become a commercially available snack. This version, contributed by Idaho cowboy poet Howard Norskog, uses venison, but beef and other game meats are often used.

Cut the meat with the grain into ¼ to ½ inch strips. For marinade, stir together Worcestershire sauce, soy sauce, salt, mustard, pepper, onion powder, and garlic powder. Place meat strips in glass dish and pour in marinade, turning strips to coat well. Cover the dish and marinate meat in refrigerator overnight.

Dry meat strips on paper towels. Place strips directly on oven racks in a single layer. Shape a "drip pan" of aluminum foil and attach it underneath the rack to keep the top layer from dripping on to the lower rack. (Also saves cleaning your oven.) Let the strips dry at 200 degrees for 6 to 8 hours. Remove the drip pan after two hours or when the meat appears to have quit dripping. Cool and store strips in a tightly sealed jar or can.

Deer Hunter's Jerky
Brown sugar
Berries or other fruit
Suet

PEMMICAN

This version of the traditional Native American food also comes from Howard Norskog, who calls it a "fabulous survival food. If rose hips were added it would be a complete food."

Let the jerky dry for up to two weeks; break it into shreds and place in a large bowl with brown sugar and berries or other fruit. Add enough suet to bind the ingredients together when mixed with hands. Form into patties and dry in a 200-degree oven. Store in plastic bags.

SADDLEBAG LUNCH COOKIES
Makes 10 dozen cookies

Marie Smith of Somers, Montana, is a rancher and cowboy poet.

In a bowl beat shortening and sugars. Beat in eggs, orange rind, and vanilla. Stir together flour, salt, baking soda, and cinnamon. Fold into creamed mixture. Add oats, nuts, raisins, and cranberries. Blend well. Roll into small balls and place on a lightly greased cookie sheet; flatten with a fork. Or, form dough into rolls of 1 ½ inch diameter and refrigerate; cut into ¼ inch slices just before baking. Bake at 350 degrees for 8 to 10 minutes or until golden.

2 cups shortening
2 cups granulated sugar
2 cups brown sugar
4 eggs
2 tablespoons grated orange rind
2 teaspoons vanilla
3 cups flour
2 teaspoons salt
2 teaspoons baking soda
2 teaspoons cinnamon
6 cups Quaker's Old Fashioned oats
2 cups chopped walnuts
1 cup raisins
1 cup chopped fresh or dried cranberries

A COWBOY'S LUNCH
Marie Smith

I didn't know until I married one,
That cowboys don't pack a lunch,
At least no respecting buckaroo
Would be caught dead with sandwich and punch. . . .

So for breakfast I cook sausage and hashbrowns,
And three eggs, yokes broke and fried hard.
My creamed oatmeal and fancy spiced peaches
I can from the tree in the yard. . . .

Even though the meal seems substantial,
I worry when noon rolls around
And wish he was closer to fix him
A picnic we can spread on the ground.

But I respect this strange cowboy reasoning,
Think my man has a will of steel,
'Til one day I bake oatmeal cookies
To serve with the evening meal.

"My favorite cookies," my cowboy says,
And he polishes off quite a few.
"Maybe I'll take some tomorrow,"
He smiles, "just to remind me of you."

Now, they are full of nourishment,
Like oatmeal and raisins and nuts,
And orange peel and cranberries
And eggs, and flour and such.
"I thought cowboys didn't eat any lunch,"
I say next morning as he takes a whole pile.
"Aw, this ain't real food, just somethin' to chaw,"
He says with a crooked smile.

I watch him tuck them out of sight
In his slickered roll of yellow,
"But you don't tell no one, you promise me?"
I nodded. "They wouldn't understand a fella

Who loves his wife so much that he
Would break the cowboy code."
"Whoever had such a loving man?"
I think, as I wave him on up the road.

So I always see there are cookies
Made of oatmeal, raisins and nuts,
So my cowboy has something to remember me by,
Though he'll swear he never eats lunch.

40 sausages such as bratwurst, kielbasa, Italian sausage, and Basque chorizo
Domestic and foreign mustards
Mayonnaise

EARLY SUMMER SAUSAGE GRILL

What better way to celebrate the coming of summer than to gather friends in a well-loved place and share good food? For the McMullen family, that place is the Lazy A-T Ranch on the South Fork of the Humboldt River, which has been our hearts' home for over thirty years. In the grove of cottonwoods that shade the ranch house, family and friends play horseshoes or chat around the cooking fire. While children armed with buckets and strainers mount expeditions into the meadows to catch frogs or hunt for nests, in the kitchen, many hands assist in the preparations. As the tempting odor of sizzling meat rises into the evening air, the clang of the dinner bell calls us from field and barn to a festive meal served on tables under the trees.

Sausages grilled over an open fire are the central feature of this menu. Many kinds of sausages were at first incorporated into ranch cooking to satisfy the tastes of cowboys of varying ethnic backgrounds, but they soon became a western staple. Here sausages are paired with homemade sandwich rolls and three tasty make-ahead salads for a meal that is hearty and appetizing.

SAUSAGE SAMPLER
Serves 20

Just prior to cooking, pierce each sausage in several places and arrange on the grill. Cook slowly, turning occasionally, while you bring out the remaining dishes.

DUDES
Nick Johnson

We were camped just under Hawk's Rest,
Me and Al and a span of Dudes,
A Lawyer out of Boston
And a Doc from Baton Rouge,
And they talked on vital subjects
Just the way them waddies will
On how to love a woman
And the way to run a still.

In the west the sun was huntin'
For a place to roll his bed,
And he had his blankets scattered
Pink and brown and orange and red
In a heap of gay profusion
Clean across the western sky,
And the little stars came peeping out
As the light began to die.

You could hear the horse bells tinkle
In the park above our camp.
And the wind came up the valley
Blowing soft and smelling damp,
And it made the campfire flicker
As it rustled thru the wood,
Mixed the odor of the flowers
With the smell of cooking food.

Then the moon sent out a detail
For to scout among the peaks.
And they fetched the shadows jumpin'
In and out like hide-and-seek.
In the east the fox was barkin'
Out derision at the moon,
A followin' up his patrol,
Rosy red, shaped like a plume.

And the Doc turned to the Lawyer
And he says, "God, ain't this dead;
Nothin' to do but sit and fidget,
Guess I'll chase myself to bed.
You can talk about Dame Nature,
But the next time that I go
For to see this wide and woolly West
I'll bring a radio."

2 cups warm water

3 tablespoons sugar

2 packages (5 teaspoons) active
    dry yeast

5 to 6 cups flour

1 ½ teaspoons salt

¼ cup olive oil

HOMEMADE DELI ROLLS
Makes 20 rolls

These rolls are best made fresh the day you serve them.

In a large bowl stir together water, sugar, and yeast. Allow to proof. In another bowl stir together 5 cups flour, and salt. Add olive oil and flour mixture to yeast mixture, 1 cup at a time, until dough is dry enough to handle. Turn onto a lightly floured board and knead until smooth and elastic, about 10 minutes. Place in greased bowl, turning to grease top. Cover and let rise in a warm place about 1 hour or until double.

Punch dough down; turn onto lightly floured board. Divide into 20 equal pieces. Form each piece into a smooth oblong, which is roughly ½ the size of the sausages; place in a greased 13x9-inch baking dish so that the sides are just touching. Cover; let rise about 45 minutes or until double.

Bake at 400 degrees 15 to 20 minutes. Cool on wire racks until ready to serve.

4 cups finely shredded green
    cabbage

⅔ cup finely shredded carrots

½ cup finely chopped green pepper

⅓ cup minced yellow onion

2 tablespoons chopped pimiento

2 tablespoons snipped parsley

⅔ cup mayonnaise

⅔ cup sour cream

1 tablespoon white vinegar

1 tablespoon fresh lemon juice

1 tablespoon prepared
    horseradish

2 to 3 teaspoons sugar

½ teaspoon salt

¼ teaspoon pepper

MEG'S COLESLAW
Serves 8

Meg Birak first introduced us to this slaw. She serves it for her annual Christmas Eve open house on sandwiches of thin-sliced corned beef and brown rye bread. It is especially good served as a garnish on the sausage rolls but just as wonderful when served as a side salad.

In a large bowl combine cabbage, carrots, green pepper, onion, pimiento, and parsley. Stir together remaining ingredients and pour over cabbage mixture. Cover and chill for at least 1 hour before serving.

THREE BEAN SALAD
Serves 6

Bean salads, a favorite of the Basque people who came to the West as ranch hands and sheepherders, were frequently eaten in line camps and camp kitchens when fresh greens weren't available. There are many recipes, some based on a medley of different beans and some on only a single variety. This one was given to me as a girl and has been a family favorite since.

Blanch fresh beans or cook frozen beans according to package directions; cool. In a large bowl combine green beans, kidney beans, garbanzo beans, onion, pimientos, and eggs. Stir together olive oil, vinegar, mustard, salt, and pepper. Pour over bean mixture, tossing to coat. Cover and chill for 2 days before serving.

1 ½ cups fresh green beans
    or one 10-ounce package frozen
    green beans
1 10-ounce can kidney beans
1 10-ounce can garbanzo beans
    (also called chickpeas)
¾ cup minced green onion
1 4-ounce jar chopped pimientos
7 hard-boiled eggs, chopped
½ cup olive oil
½ cup red wine vinegar
⅓ cup Dijon-style mustard
1 ½ teaspoons salt
1 teaspoon pepper

PASTA SALAD
Serves 10

In a large bowl combine rigatoni, onion, olives, red pepper, celery, and artichoke hearts. Stir together reserved oil from artichoke hearts, vinegar, olive oil, salt, and pepper to taste. Pour over pasta mixture. Stir in mayonnaise. Cover and chill till serving time.

8 cups rigatoni, cooked and cooled
½ cup finely chopped red onion
½ cup sliced black olives
½ cup finely chopped red pepper
½ cup thinly sliced celery
2 7-ounce jars marinated artichoke
    hearts, drained (reserve oil)
½ cup red wine vinegar
¼ cup olive oil
½ teaspoon salt
Fresh ground pepper
¾ cup mayonnaise

SOFT GINGER BREAD
Serves 9

In a bowl stir together flour, ginger, cinnamon, and cloves. Set aside. In another bowl beat butter with an electric mixer till softened. Add sugar and beat till fluffy. Beat in molasses. Dissolve baking soda in water. Slowly add soda and water, beating on low speed. Slowly add flour mixture and beat until smooth. Add the beaten eggs. Pour into a greased and floured 9x9-inch baking pan. Bake at 325 degrees for 45 to 50 minutes. Cut into 3-inch squares and serve hot from the oven or cooled. Top with sweetened whipped cream.

To serve a group of 20, bake two recipes, but be sure to use two 9x9 pans.

2 ½ cups flour
1 teaspoon ground ginger
1 teaspoon ground cinnamon
1 teaspoon ground cloves
½ cup butter or margarine
1 cup sugar
2 teaspoons baking soda
1 cup boiling water
½ cup molasses
2 eggs, well beaten
1 cup heavy cream, whipped and
    sweetened to taste

MENU

PANTRY SOUP

MYRA'S HEARTH BREAD

LETTUCE, RAISIN, AND WALNUT SALAD WITH CREAMY BASIL DRESSING

SLICED ORANGES WITH SHERRY

BETTE'S SHORTBREADS

3 small or 2 large boneless chicken
    breast halves, diced
2 tablespoons cooking oil
½ cup chopped onion
1 large clove garlic, pressed
1 large carrot, sliced
½ cup sliced mushrooms
3 10 ½-ounce cans chicken broth
1 10 ½ -ounce can stewed tomatoes
1 10-ounce can garbanzo beans or kidney
    beans
1 can water
¾ cup sliced celery
½ cup white wine
1 teaspoon dried basil
1 cup pasta (rotelle or rigatoni are best)
Pepper
Grated Parmesan cheese

LATE NIGHT SOUP SUPPER

The sun has dropped below the line of western hills as we ride down the lane toward the house, dark and silent in its stand of cottonwoods. Our horses, quiet after the long ride, pick up the pace as they sense the nearness of the barn and the long, cool meadow behind it.

The workday has been a family affair, the four of us pushing cattle from one large summer pasture into the next, where the crested wheat is thick and green. Dust and sun, a gulp of tepid water from a canteen slung over the saddlehorn, quick, jolting rides through sagebrush after a breechy cow—these mark days in the saddle.

We are bone-weary, but the chores must be done, the stock fed. My father, brother and I unsaddle the horses and reward them with pans of oats before we turn them out to roll their sweaty saddle marks away. We move slowly, thinking not of food, but of sleep. But as we finish, the lighted kitchen coaxes us in and we are tantalized by the aroma of Mom's bubbling quick soup wrapped all around with yeasty hot bread. No food ever tasted as good as this simple meal shared around that wide table after a day of working together.

PANTRY SOUP
Serves 4

This soup is quickly prepared with ingredients on hand. It adapts easily to leftover rice, a few garden-fresh green beans, or a handful of peas. If you get home late, you can thaw the chicken in your microwave oven for 1 to 2 minutes before dicing.

In a large Dutch oven brown chicken pieces in hot oil. Add onion and garlic and stir briefly. Add mushrooms and stir until tender. Add broth, tomatoes, beans, water, celery, wine, and basil. Bring to boiling; reduce heat. Simmer until vegetables are tender, but crisp. Add pasta and continue simmering until pasta is tender. Season with pepper. Serve with Parmesan cheese.

SUNDOWN IN THE COW CAMP
Joel Nelson

The hoodie's washed the dishes
And stacked 'em in the box;
The old cook and the foreman
Have wound and set their clocks.

That horseshoe game they're playin'
Hasta shut down in a while,
'Cause that shadow from the outhouse
Reaches dang near half a mile.

Ol' Charlie's got his guitar out;
That Charlie sure can play.
And it's sundown in the cow camp—
It's my favorite time o' day.

We ate at five this mornin'
'Cept the "Kid"—he skipped his chuck.
He just couldn't eat fer knowin'
That this mornin' horse would buck.

Now the cook has shut the chuck-box lid
And gave the fire a poke,
Throwed some coals around the coffee pot
And lit his evenin' smoke.

His expression kinda clues you
That his memories have flown
To other camps at sundown
And the cowboys that he's known.

The Kid has kept a night horse up;
He's down there in the pens;
Just plumb forgot about his feed;
He's nickerin' fer his friends.

Those calves we worked and turned back out
Have purt'neer mothered up;
Just one cow left a bawlin'.
Think I'll have me one last cup.

You can feel the breeze is shiftin'
Like a cool front's on the way.
Glad the sun's been busy warmin' up
My teepee tent all day.

Some cowboys turn in early—
The cook's the first to go—
While the night owls hug the coffee pot
Till the fire's a dull red glow.

You'll hear it all around the fire—
Poems, politics and song,
Solutions for the price of beef,
Where the BLM went wrong.

That strong and silent cowboy type—
The one you read about—
He's kinda forced to be that way
When the drive's all scattered out.

But he'll get downright eloquent
When the evening chuck's washed down,
And it's sunset in the cow camp,
With the crew gathered 'round.

Half asleep here in my bedroll,
I can hear those night owls laugh;
But that old cow's stopped her bawlin',
So I guess she's found her calf.

Myra's Hearth Bread
Makes 1 loaf

In a large bowl stir together yeast and sugar; add warm milk. Allow to proof. Meanwhile, combine 1 cup of the unbleached flour, the whole-wheat flour, and salt. Add flour mixture to yeast mixture. Beat vigorously for approximately five minutes. Stir in another ½ cup unbleached flour and turn dough onto lightly floured board. Using remaining flour, knead until bread is smooth, elastic and bounces back when pressed. This will take approximately 10 minutes. Shape into an oval loaf.

Sprinkle cornmeal over a baking sheet and place the loaf on the cornmeal. Cover and let rise about 1 hour. Use a sharp knife and slash top of risen dough crosswise. Bake at 350 degrees about 1 hour or until nicely browned.

While bread is baking, in a small saucepan stir together cold water and cornstarch. Cook and stir till thickened and bubbly. Brush top of bread with cornstarch mixture after it has baked 10 minutes; brush again after 25 minutes.

This recipe adapts well to sourdough too. Just leave out the yeast and the milk and substitute two cups of sourdough starter. Add the flour to the starter and allow it to work an hour or more before adding the salt and sugar.

1 package (2 ½ teaspoons)
  dry yeast
1 teaspoon sugar
1 cup milk, scalded and cooled
2 cups unbleached flour
1 cup whole wheat flour
1 teaspoon salt
1 tablespoon butter or margarine
3 tablespoons cornmeal
½ cup cold water
1 teaspoon cornstarch

Lettuce, Raisin, and Walnut Salad with Creamy Basil Dressing

Stir together buttermilk, sour cream, mayonnaise, milk, basil, and lemon juice. Cover and chill till serving time. Just before serving, toss together greens, walnuts, raisins, and avocado. Pour basil mixture over greens mixture, tossing to coat.

¼ cup buttermilk
¼ cup sour cream
¼ cup mayonnaise
¼ cup milk or light cream
¼ cup fresh basil leaves, snipped
2 ½ tablespoons fresh lemon juice
2 handfuls mixed greens
½ cup toasted walnuts
½ cup raisins
1 ripe avocado, peeled, pitted, and
  chopped

SLICED ORANGES WITH SHERRY
Serves 4

4 oranges
¼ cup dry sherry
2 tablespoons powdered sugar

Peel oranges, removing as much of the white membrane as possible. Slice ¼ inch thick. Arrange on 4 individual salad plates. Stir together dry sherry and powdered sugar. Pour over oranges and serve.

BETTE'S SHORTBREADS
Makes approximately 3 dozen 2-inch cookies

½ cup packed brown sugar
½ cup granulated sugar
1 pound butter, softened
1 egg, at room temperature
4 cups flour
Pinch salt
Dash baking soda

In a bowl beat butter or margarine on medium speed till softened. Add sugars and beat till light and fluffy. Beat in egg. Continue beating while adding the flour, soda, and salt. (Some of the flour may have to be added by hand.) Chill. Shape into half-dollar size rounds and bake at 275 degrees for 20 minutes. These cookies will keep for several weeks in an air-tight container in the refrigerator. They make a wonderful hostess gift.

Katherine Field - 35.

MENU

BRAISED LAMB SHANKS AND BEANS

SHEEPHERDER'S BREAD

MIXED GREENS AND AVOCADO SALAD WITH GARLIC DRESSING

RICE PUDDING

BARNEY'S BASQUE LAMB DINNER

Feuds between ranchers and sheepmen are part of the mythology of the West. Cowboy poems and songs refer to sheep in scornful tones as "woollies." Yet lamb has long been a staple food in the West, and the people called Basques from the Pyrenees Mountains of France and Spain became some of the best ranch cooks.

Most Basques emigrated to the western states in the early 1900s. They entered the United States on work permits as sheepherders—not because they were herders in the old country, but because they were willing to work long days alone in the mountains with only a dog or two and thousands of sheep for company. Ranch people admired their hardworking ways and their flare for food. Many Basques were hired on as chuckwagon cooks, where their simple style easily adapted to the Dutch oven and the open fire.

This menu is named in honor of Barney Monasterio, Basque cook at the 71 Ranch at Halleck, Nevada, during my father's tenure there as ranch manager. Barney's cure for any ill—from the common cold to thumb-sucking—was some form of garlic: garlic soup or raw garlic wrapped in bread and washed down with milk. He cooked by instinct rather than measurement; we have never been able to recreate the light, sweet corn fritters he was famous for. The table in Barney's kitchen was lined with cowboys, drummers, passersby—and the owners of area ranches who always tried to hire him away. The dishes that follow honor Barney's method, turning humble ingredients (lamb shanks, beans, rice, garlic) into a memorable meal.

THE DUTCH OVEN
Bruce Kiskaddon

You mind that old oven so greasy and black,
That we hauled in a wagon or put in a pack.
The biscuits she baked wasn't bad by no means,
And she had the world cheated fer cookin' up beans.
If the oven was there you could always git by,
You could bake, you could boil, you could stew, you could fry.

When the fire was built she was throwed in to heat
While they peeled the potaters and cut down the meat.
Then the cook put some fire down into a hole.
Next, he set in the oven and put on some coals.
I allus remember the way the cook did
When he took the old "Goncho" and lifted the lid.

He really was graceful at doin' the trick.
The old greasy sackers they just used a stick.
Boy Howdy! We all made a gen'l attack
If the hoss with the dutch oven scattered his pack.
You mind how you lifted your hoss to a lope
And built a long loop in the end of your rope.

You bet them old waddies knowed what to expect.
No biscuits no more if that oven got wrecked.
We didn't know much about prayin' or lovin'
But I reckon we worshiped that greasy old oven.
And the old cowboy smiles when his memory drifts back
To the oven that rode in the wagon or pack.

2 tablespoons cooking oil
6 meaty lamb shanks
1 28-ounce can whole tomatoes,
   drained
1 onion, chopped
1 carrot, sliced
1 celery stalk, sliced
2 cloves garlic, minced
1 cup red wine
½ cup double-strength beef broth
   (if using canned do not dilute)
1 teaspoon dried thyme
½ teaspoon salt
¼ teaspoon pepper
1 cup dried white beans, washed
   and soaked
1 celery stalk, chopped
¼ cup chopped onion
1 bay leaf
Fresh parsley, minced

3 cups very hot water
½ cup butter or margarine
½ cup sugar
2 ½ teaspoons salt
1 package dry yeast
9 ½ cups unbleached flour

BRAISED LAMB SHANKS AND BEANS
Serves 6

For a more elegant presentation you can substitute a leg of lamb for the shanks but we like the fuller, more distinctive flavor of the shanks. Serve with a full-bodied Zinfandel or California Cabernet Sauvignon.

Heat oil in a large Dutch oven over medium-high heat. Add lamb and brown on all sides. Remove from pan. Drain off fat. Place tomatoes, onion, carrot, celery, and garlic in Dutch oven. Arrange shanks over vegetables. Add wine, broth, thyme, salt and pepper. Cover and bake at 325 degrees for 2 hours.

Place beans in a medium saucepan; add enough water just to cover. Add celery, chopped onion, and bay leaf. Bring to boiling; reduce heat. Cover and simmer until the beans begin to feel tender.

When the beans are nearly cooked, drain and add them to the lamb shanks. Bake for 1 hour more.

To serve, arrange the shanks on a warmed platter. Place in a low oven to keep warm. Drain beans, reserving liquid. Spoon beans around the lamb and return to oven to keep warm. Skim fat from reserved liquid and add salt and pepper to taste. Pour approximately ½ cup of the reserved liquid over the lamb and bean mixture. Sprinkle the platter with fresh parsley. Serve with remaining liquid.

SHEEPHERDER'S BREAD
Makes 1 large loaf

This traditional Basque bread was often prepared in Dutch ovens and baked on hot coals in the ground. The sheep-camp cook would prepare the bread early in the day and then leave it to bake, covered with coals, until he returned after morning chores. This recipe from Anita Mitchell has appeared in several local publications and is recognized as one of the most successful and authentic renditions of this classic bread.

In a bowl combine water, butter or margarine, sugar, and salt. Stir until butter melts. Cool to 110 to 115 degrees. Add yeast; cover and let stand for 15 minutes in a warm place.

Add 5 cups of the flour. Mix with a wooden spoon to form a thick batter. With the spoon, stir in remaining flour to form a stiff dough.

Turn the dough onto a floured board and knead about 10 minutes or until smooth, adding another cup of flour as needed to prevent sticking. Place dough in a greased bowl and turn to coat. Let rise about 1½ hours or until doubled. Punch down and knead on a floured board to form a smooth ball.

Cut a circle of foil to cover the bottom of a heavy Dutch oven (approximately 10 inches in diameter). Grease the inside of the oven and the underside of the lid with cooking oil. Place the dough in the oven and cover with the lid. Let rise in a warm place until the dough pushes the lid up about ½" (Yes it will!) This will take about 1 hour. Watch it carefully.

When the lid has lifted, bake the covered bread in a 375 degree oven for 12 minutes. Remove the lid and continue to bake for 30 to 35 minutes more. The loaf should be golden brown and sound hollow when thumped on the top with your knuckles. Remove the cooked loaf from the oven and turn out onto a rack to cool.

MIXED GREENS AND AVOCADO SALAD WITH GARLIC DRESSING
Serves 6

For dressing, stir together oil, vinegar, salt, Accent, pepper, and garlic. Cover and chill for several hours. Prepare salad by combining lettuce, avocado, mushrooms, onions, and almonds. Just before serving, pour dressing over greens, tossing to coat. Sprinkle with fresh ground pepper.

½ cup olive oil
¼ cup tarragon vinegar
2 teaspoons salt
2 teaspoons Accent seasoning
¼ teaspoon black pepper
2 large cloves garlic, crushed
1 head read leaf lettuce, torn
1 head butter lettuce, torn
1 avocado, peeled, pitted, and chopped
5 medium mushrooms, sliced
2 green onions, sliced
½ cup sliced almonds
Fresh ground pepper

RICE PUDDING
Serves 6

In a saucepan heat milk until tiny bubbles appear around edges of the saucepan. Sprinkle rice and salt over the milk. Add cinnamon stick and cover saucepan. Place saucepan in a baking dish which has been filled with water to a depth of 2 inches. Bake at 325 degrees for 1 hour and 35 minutes or until very creamy. Remove from oven and add sugar. Pour into a shallow dish which has been rinsed in cold water. Sprinkle ground cinnamon over top. Cool pudding, stirring every 20 minutes. It will continue to thicken and rice will continue to expand while it cools.

½ gallon milk
¾ cup short grain rice
½ teaspoon salt
1 cinnamon stick
¾ cup sugar
¼ teaspoon ground cinnamon

MENU

VENISON STEAKS WITH SECRET BUTTER SAUCE

GRILLED RED POTATOES WITH SOUR CREAM

JANE'S CARROTS IN BASIL BUTTER

ROMAINE AND PINE NUT SALAD

CONTINENTAL BREAD

GRANDMA'S DREAM COOKIES

BLACKBERRY SORBET

6 venison steaks, preferably cut from the loin
6 tablespoons butter or margarine
1 teaspoon Worcestershire sauce
3 tablespoons sliced green onions

VENISON FEAST

Mule deer and cattle coexist on the ranges of the West as they always have since the first cattle herds were trailed north and west into the new territories. It is a common sight to look out across a long sweep of field in the morning or evening and see the elusive shapes of grazing deer mingled with the red or black Hereford or Angus cattle.

In hard winters, deer come down from the mountains to share the hay spread for cattle. Most ranchers don't mind; perhaps they identify with the deer's independence, its ability to ignore the barbed wire boundaries which have domesticated so much of the West. But when a cowboy or rancher bags a deer, he does so with a stoic respect for the cycle of life and death played out in a harsh environment.

The taste of venison combines a bit of sagebrush, the crispness of mountain air, and a hint of earth.

VENISON STEAKS WITH SECRET BUTTER SAUCE
Serves 6

The secret to good venison steaks is not to overcook them; they should be served very rare.

Grill steaks over hot coals approximately 4 minutes per side. Meanwhile, in a small saucepan combine butter, green onions, and Worcestershire sauce. Place saucepan on the side of the grill or on the stove over low heat till melted. As soon as the steaks are ready, remove them to a platter and pour half the butter mixture over all. Keep remaining sauce warm. If bones are not a problem, slice diagonally into ¼-inch slices. If slicing isn't possible, cut meat into serving-size pieces. Pour remaining butter sauce over the top and serve.

MESSAGE IN THE WIND
Jesse Smith

As you set and look from the ridge,
    To the valley of green down below,
You reach up and pull down yer lid,
    As a cool wind starts to blow.

Yer old pony's eyes are a-lookin',
    His ears workin' forward and back.
All of a sudden you feel his hide tighten,
    And a little hump come into his back.

That hoss's a readin' a message,
    That's been sent to him in the breeze.
You feel yer gut start to tighten,
    And a shakin' come into yer knees.

Ya look to the right and see nothin',
    Ya look to the left, it's the same.
Except for the birds, rabbits, and squirrels,
    And two hawks a-playin' a game.

But you know yer old hoss ain't a-lying,
    He's as good'ne as you'll ever find.
And you know that old pony's tryin'
    To warn ya 'bout somethin' in time.

Well, ya look real hard where he's lookin',
    His eyes are plum fixed in a stare,
Then ya see what he's seein',
    A cub and an old mama bear.

The trail you'd a took went between them,
    That old mama bear'd a got tough.
That old pony like as not saved yer hide,
    Or a life-shortenin' scare, shor-a-nuff.

You watch 'em go 'cross the meadow,
    And ya ride on yer way once again,
And ya shor thank the Lord for the message,
    He sent to yer hoss on the wind.

2 pounds small red potatoes
1 ½ cups water
½ teaspoon salt
¼ cup olive oil
2 clove garlics, mashed
½ teaspoon freshly ground pepper
Sour cream

GRILLED RED POTATOES WITH SOUR CREAM
Serves 6

Scrub potatoes and place in a casserole dish with water and salt. Cover and cook in a microwave oven on high heat for 8 to 10 minutes or till potatoes are just tender. Or, steam potatoes over boiling water till just tender. Drain potatoes; set aside.

In the same dish, combine olive oil, garlic, and pepper. Return potatoes to the dish, tossing to coat with oil mixture. (Potatoes can be prepared ahead to this point and let sit in the oil and garlic as long as 6 to 8 hours.)

Thread the potatoes on metal or bamboo skewers so potatoes just touch each other. Place the skewers over the coals. Turn them every three minutes and brush with the reserved oil until evenly browned. If your grill isn't large enough, these potatoes can be steamed until tender, then rolled in pressed garlic and butter and sprinkled with fresh chopped parsley. Serve with sour cream.

2 pounds baby carrots
¼ cup butter or margarine
¼ cup chopped fresh basil
¼ teaspoon salt
⅛ teaspoon fresh ground pepper

JANE'S CARROTS IN BASIL BUTTER
Serves 6

Wash and steam carrots until tender. In a medium skillet melt butter; add carrots, basil, salt, and pepper. Stir until carrots are well coated.

2 heads romaine lettuce
⅓ cup vegetable oil
⅓ cup garlic oil
¼ cup olive oil
1 tablespoon Worcestershire sauce
1 egg, beaten
3 lemons, juiced
¾ cup croutons
¾ cup toasted pine nuts
½ cup freshly grated Romano
    cheese
2 teaspoons freshly ground pepper

ROMAINE AND PINE NUT SALAD
Serves 6

To make garlic oil, chop or mash enough garlic to cover 1 inch of a pint crock. Fill with salad oil or light olive oil. Cover and store at room temperature for several months. Use oil only.

Prepare the lettuce by removing the outer leaves and washing the remaining heads. Shake dry, wrap in a kitchen towel, and place in the lower portion of the refrigerator to crisp.

In a large salad bowl, combine vegetable oil, garlic oil, olive oil, and Worcestershire sauce. Add lettuce and egg, tossing to coat. Add lemon juice. Sprinkle with croutons, pine nuts, and cheese. Toss well.

CONTINENTAL BREAD
Makes 1 large or 2 small loaves

1 ½ packages (3 ¾ teaspoons)
   active dry yeast
1 tablespoon sugar
2 cups warm water
5 tablespoons olive oil
1 tablespoon salt
6 to 6 ½ cups bread flour
1 tablespoon egg white, mixed with 1
   tablespoon cold water

In a large bowl combine yeast and sugar; stir in warm water. Allow to proof (about 10 minutes). Add the oil and stir. Add flour and salt to the yeast mixture, one cup at a time, until you have a stiff dough. Remove to a lightly floured board and knead about 10 minutes or until stiff and smooth. Place in a well oiled or buttered bowl, turn to coat, and allow to rise for 1½ to 2 hours or until doubled. Punch down. Knead lightly and return to bowl to rise, about 1½ hours.

Punch down and shape into 1 large or 2 small loaves. Place in bread pan(s) and allow to rise about 20 minutes. Slash top in two or three places. Bake at 400 degrees for 35 minutes. Brush with egg white mixture and bake for 10 minutes more or till well browned.

GRANDMA'S DREAM COOKIES

½ cup butter, softened
½ cup margarine, softened
½ cup sugar
1 egg yolk
1 teaspoon vanilla
2 ¼ cups flour
Walnut halves

In a bowl beat butter and margarine with an electric mixer till softened. Add sugar and beat till light and fluffy. Add egg yolk and vanilla; beat till well combined. Gradually beat in flour. Mix well, using your hands if dough is too stiff for your mixer. On a lightly floured surface, roll dough ⅛ inch thick. Cut into rounds using the top of a small drinking glass which has been dipped in flour. Or, shape dough into a roll, wrap in waxed paper, and store in the freezer. As you need cookies, thaw dough slightly and cut into ⅛ inch thick slices. Place a walnut half in the center of each cookie. Bake at 400 degrees for 5 to 6 minutes.

BLACKBERRY SORBET
Serves 4

4 to 6 cups frozen blackberries
6 tablespoons sugar
1 ¾ cups water
2 tablespoons blackberry brandy
1 tablespoon brandy

This sorbet is made with a food processor and requires none of the fuss of an ice cream freezer.

In a saucepan combine the berries, water, and sugar. Bring to a boil, stirring to dissolve the sugar. Reduce heat and simmer for 1 hour. Remove from the heat and strain through a fine sieve or cheese cloth. Stir in the blackberry brandy and brandy. Pour the mixture into an 8x8-inch baking pan and freeze for 1 hour. Pour partially frozen mixture into a food processor. Cover and pulse processor 6 to 8 times. Pour back into baking pan and freeze for another hour; process as before. Continue the freezing and processing until the sorbet reaches a very slushy consistency. This will require a total of four or five hours. Return it to the freezer until ready to serve.

This recipe can also be prepared in a traditional ice cream freezer according to the manufacturer's instructions.

MENU

STEAMED ARTICHOKES

HERBED TURKEY

PASTA WITH FOUR CHEESES

ASPARAGUS IN SESAME BUTTER

SPINACH SALAD WITH RASPBERRY VINAIGRETTE

QUICK FRENCH BREAD

LEMON TART

10 small to medium artichokes, washed and trimmed
2 tablespoons red wine vinegar
1 teaspoon salt
1 teaspoon garlic powder
½ teaspoon dried oregano
½ teaspoon olive oil
Mayonnaise
Lemon butter

WOODSTOVE TURKEY DINNER

The little black wood stove is the heart of our ranch kitchen. It warms us and heats our coffee on chilly mornings, it dries our clothes drenched in a sudden rainstorm, and it always holds a simmering pot or two, sending wonderful smells into every corner of the house. This little stove is also a center of memories: bedding down a leppy calf in the kitchen and feeding it warm milk from a pop bottle; sniffing a bubbling pot of red chokecherry juice; filling the house with smoke when I forgot to open the chimney draft.

Woodstove cooking is tricky. Each stove has its quirks, its hot and cold spots. Some kinds of wood burn hotter than others. And the hardest lesson for a modern cook: you must remember to stoke the fire often, or it will go out.

Yet foods cooked on a wood stove have a flavor that no modern stove can duplicate. The skin of our Woodstove Turkey crisps in the smoky heat of the oven, the meat underneath tender and flavored with fresh herbs. We serve this summer turkey unstuffed, with homemade pasta topped with cheeses and a fresh tomato and basil salsa. With practice, every dish in this menu can be prepared on a wood stove, but we have provided cooking instructions for the modern range and microwave.

STEAMED ARTICHOKES
Serves 10

Arrange 4 or 5 of the artichokes in a microwave-safe dish. Stir together vinegar, salt, garlic powder, oregano, and oil; pour half of the mixture over the artichokes. Microwave on high power for 10 to 15 minutes until an inner leaf from each artichoke pulls out easily. Remove the cooked artichokes to a plate to drain. Repeat with the remaining artichokes and vinegar mixture. To serve, place each artichoke in the center of a serving plate with 2 tablespoons mayonnaise and a small cup of lemon butter.

COWDOGS
Ed Brown

Now some cowdogs have pedigrees
　　And other claims to fame.
But here a cowdog gets two things:
　　A whipping and a name.

And we don't just give them a name
　　From a book upon the shelves.
We use them, and if they stay around,
　　We let them name themselves.

Now Lucky got his easily,
　　We didn't like the sound.
He just hopped in the pickup truck
　　While I was at the pound.

And Romeo, he's not much show;
　　His usefulness is slim.
But all the pups for miles around
　　Look exactly like him.

Just how O' Screech got his name,
　　I bet I beat you to it—
It's the sound that a fence makes
　　When he's running cattle through it.

With Ornery's disposition you'd not
　　Give him half a chance,
But he does come in handy
　　Keeping salesmen off the ranch.

Some of the names that we've bestowed
　　Don't need much explanation;
Meter Maid marks tires, and
　　Lazy's on vacation.

Backhoe fills the yard with holes;
　　Nixon covers them up;
Welfare hasn't done a thing
　　Since he was just a pup.

Buzzard eats the darndest things;
　　Leppie's mother never claimed him.
If we had a dog that could work cows
　　We wouldn't know what to name him.

KatherineField . 94

53

1 15-pound turkey
1 cup chicken stock
1 garlic clove, minced
1 teaspoon dried basil
1 teaspoon salt
1 teaspoon dried thyme
½ teaspoon ground pepper
½ teaspoon dried rosemary
½ teaspoon dried marjoram
1 cup unsalted butter
1 ½ cups dry white wine

HERBED TURKEY
Serves 10

Wash turkey, pat dry inside and out. Preheat oven to 325 degrees. Grease roasting rack and pan. Pour ½ cup chicken stock into roasting pan. Combine garlic, basil, salt, thyme, pepper, rosemary, and marjoram. Gently lift skin from breast area of turkey and spread with ⅓ of herb mixture. Secure skin with skewers and spread with ¼ cup of the butter. Sprinkle remaining herb mixture evenly over turkey. Tie legs and wings as needed. Place turkey, breast side down, on rack and roast for 30 minutes. Melt remaining butter; add wine. Baste turkey generously with the butter and wine after the first 30 minutes of roasting. Continue to baste with remaining butter and wine and pan juices every 20 to 30 minutes adding remaining ½ cup of stock as needed. Allow 15 to 18 minutes cooking time per pound. During the last hour of roasting, carefully turn the turkey breast-side up. Continue basting every 20 minutes. If turkey gets too brown during roasting, cover loosely with a foil tent. Let stand 15 minutes before carving.

3 pounds tomatoes, cored, seeded
   and coarsely chopped
¾ cup fresh basil, shredded
1 ½ teaspoons salt
2 large cloves garlic, minced
12 ounces ricotta cheese at room
   temperature
3 ounces fontina cheese, cut into
   ¼ inch cubes
3 ounces fresh mozzarella cheese,
   cut into ¼ inch cubes
4 tablespoons whipping cream
Freshly ground pepper
Grated nutmeg
1 ½ pounds rigatoni or rotelle
2 tablespoons olive oil
1 cup freshly grated Parmesan
   cheese

PASTA WITH FOUR CHEESES
Serves 10

In a bowl stir together tomatoes, basil, salt and garlic; set aside for several hours, stirring occasionally. In another bowl combine ricotta cheese, fontina cheese, mozzarella cheese, and cream. Add pepper and nutmeg. Set aside.

Just before serving, place pasta in boiling water with olive oil and cook to just al dente. It is very important that you don't overcook the pasta.

Toss cooked noodles with the cheese mixture and half of the Parmesan cheese; pour onto a large platter. Sprinkle with some of the remaining Parmesan cheese. If tomatoes have a lot of juice, drain and spoon the mixture into the center of the pasta platter. Serve with remaining Parmesan cheese.

ASPARAGUS WITH SESAME BUTTER
Serves 10

Cut asparagus diagonally into bite-size pieces. Place in a microwave-safe dish with 1 inch water and cook on high heat for 4 minutes, turning halfway through the cooking. Drain and rinse in cold water to stop cooking. In a large skillet melt butter and stir in lemon juice, sesame seeds, and oil. Season with salt and pepper to taste. Add asparagus pieces, tossing to coat. Transfer to a heated serving dish.

2 ½ pounds asparagus
¼ cup butter
2 tablespoons lemon juice
2 tablespoons sesame seeds, lightly toasted
2 teaspoons olive oil
Salt
Pepper

SPINACH SALAD WITH RASPBERRY VINAIGRETTE
Serves 10

For dressing, stir together oil, vinegar, salt, and pepper. In a salad bowl toss together spinach, onion, mushrooms, cheese and avocadoes. Pour the dressing over the salad and serve immediately.

⅔ cup olive oil
½ cup raspberry vinegar
¼ teaspoon salt
⅛ teaspoon pepper
2 bunches fresh spinach, washed and trimmed
1 small red onion, sliced
8 ounces fresh mushrooms, sliced
1 cup crumbled blue cheese
2 ripe avocados, peeled, pitted, and chunked

2 packages (5 teaspoons) rapid
   rise yeast
2 ¼ cups warm water
6 cups unbleached flour
1 teaspoon salt
Cornmeal

QUICK FRENCH BREAD
Makes 2 loaves

This bread can be prepared, start to finish, in 2 ½ hours.

Place yeast in the bottom of a food processor fitted with a dough blade. Add ¼ cup of the warm water and, using your hands, turn the dough blade back and forth several times to mix the yeast and water. Add 5 cups of the flour to the bowl. Turn the processor on and add the salt through the feed tube. With the machine still running, pour the remaining water through the feed tube. The dough will form a ball almost immediately. Stop the processor and check the dough. If it is too sticky, add a small amount of flour and process to combine. Be sure not to add too much.

Remove the dough to a floured board and knead lightly. Form it into a ball and place in a greased bowl. Cover lightly and let rise in a warm place until double.

Turn the dough onto the board and punch down. Using your hands roll the dough into a long oval. Cut the dough in half lengthwise. Gently lift and roll the dough to the center, leaving the top smooth and slightly twisting the undersides. This should produce a French bread shape.

Place the loaves on an ungreased cookie sheet, sprinkled with a thin layer of cornmeal. Cover and allow dough to rise for 5 to 10 minutes, until bread is well shaped. With a razor blade or sharp knife, cut 3 diagonal slits across the top of each loaf. Place in a preheated 400 degree oven and place three or four ice cubes on the bottom of your oven. (This creates the good crust.) After 10 minutes, reduce the temperature to 350 degrees and continue baking for 30 minutes.

You can usually tell from the color of the crust when this bread is done. It should be golden brown and sound hollow when tapped. Remove to a cooling rack until ready to serve. This bread does not freeze well.

LEMON TART

Pastry

Place the flour in a food processor. Process for 30 seconds and add the sugar. Process till combined. Cut the butter into several pieces and place it in the processor. Pulse the processor several times until the butter and flour resemble coarse crumbs.

In a bowl, whisk together the egg yolks and heavy cream. Turn on the processor and add the cream mixture through the feed tube. The flour will gather quickly. Be sure to stop the processor as soon as a ball has formed. Overprocessing will result in a tough and dry crust. If the dough seems too dry and will not gather, add extra cream, a little at a time.

Turn the dough onto a lightly floured surface and work the dough by rubbing it with the heel of your hand. Push down on the dough and turn your hand a quarter of a turn. Repeat this procedure until all the dough has been worked. Separate the dough into 2 equal pieces and wrap in clear plastic wrap. Refrigerate at least 2 hours before using. You will only need 1 portion of dough for this tart. The remaining dough can be frozen.

Just before preparing the filling, remove the dough from the refrigerator and pat it into a tart pan, working from the center out.

Return the prepared pan to the refrigerator for 30 minutes. Then line the pan with parchment paper, fill with pie weights, and bake at 400 degrees for 15 minutes or until lightly browned. Remove and place on a cooling rack.

2 ¾ cups flour
⅓ cup sugar
1 cup unsalted butter
2 egg yolks
¼ cup whipping cream

Filling

Place the lemon and lime peel in 2 bouquet garni bags and tie securely. In a large sauce pan or top of a double boiler, combine lemon juice, lime juice, the bags of peel, eggs, egg yolks, and sugar. Cook over medium heat, stirring constantly, until mixture comes to a boil. Filling should be smooth and very thick. Remove the pan from the heat and beat in the butter, 1 teaspoon at a time, with a wire whisk. Pour the filling into the prepared pastry shell and refrigerate. Serve with whipped cream.

⅓ cup shredded lemon peel
⅓ cup shredded lime peel
1 cup lemon juice
1 cup lime juice
6 eggs, beaten
6 egg yolks, beaten
1½ cups sugar
1 cup butter or margarine
Sweetened whipped cream

2 cups sweet and sour mix
9 ounces tequilla
6 ounces white triple sec
4 ounces Roses' lime juice
Ice
Fresh strawberries

FAJITA FIESTA

The influence of Mexico marks the maps of the American West: San Francisco, Sierra Nevada, Colorado, Rio Grande. Cowboys call their gear by Spanish words: mecate, reata, tapideros, chaps, romal. They herd cattle into corrals, ride broncos or mustangs through landscapes of mesquite or cholla, go to rodeos on holidays.

The foods of Mexico and the southwest were adopted into the cowboy tradition at the time of the trail drives. Cowboys liked the hearty tastes, the spiciness, the simple preparation. Chili has become synonymous with cowboy cooking for some people.

This menu has a modern flair, but it honors the West's appreciation of Mexican-style food. Fajitas, warm flour tortillas filled with grilled marinated meats and condiments, are commonly made of beef; our version uses chicken. The ubiquitous pinto bean moves aside for frijoles refritos made with black beans. But the spirit of western eating is preserved. Invite your guests early for margaritas and spicy appetizer dips while they help chop vegetables and fruits for the condiments and salads. Finish the meal with the smooth caramel custard called flan. Muy bueno!

MARGARITAS
Fills 1 blender

In a blender container combine sweet and sour mix, tequilla, triple sec, and lime juice. Add ice to fill container. Cover and blend on high speed until mixture is thick and slushy. Garnish each glass with a fresh strawberry.

HELL IN TEXAS
Anonymous

The Devil in Hades we're told was chained,
And there for a thousand years remained.
He did not grumble nor did he groan,
But determined to make a hell of his own
Where he could torture the souls of men
Without being chained in that poisoned pen.

So he asked the Lord if he had on hand
Anything left when he made the land.
The Lord said, "Yes, I have lots on hand,
But I left it down on the Rio Grande."

So the Devil went down and looked at the stuff,
And said if it comes as a gift he'd be stuck
For after examining it carefully and well,
He found it was too dry for Hell.

So in order to get it off'n his hands
The Lord promised the Devil to water the land,
For he had some water, or rather some dregs,
That smelled just like a case of bad eggs.
So the deal was made and the deed was given
And the Lord went back to his home in Heaven.
"Now," says the Devil, "I have all that's needed
To make a good Hell," and thus he succeeded.

He put thorns on the cactus and horns on the toads
And scattered tarantulas along the road.
He gave spiral springs to the bronco steed
And a thousand legs to the centipede. . . .

The sandburs prevail and so do the ants,
And those who sit down need half soles on their pants.
Oh, the wild boar roams the black chaparral,
It's a hell of a place he's got for Hell.

The red pepper grows on the banks of the brooks,
The Mexicans use them in all that they cook.
Just dine with the Mexican, you'll be sure to shout
From hell on the inside as well as the out.

SPECIAL GUACAMOLE

This recipe came from Amarillo, Texas, via poet Buck Ramsey's wife, Betty. She recommends that you select avocadoes with thick, bumpy skins.

In a bowl mash the avocadoes; stir in lime juice and green onions. Set aside. In a separate bowl combine the garlic and picante. Just before serving stir picante mixture into avocado mixture. Season with salt. Serve with a variety of corn chips.

4 large ripe avocadoes, peeled, and pitted
2 tablespoons lime juice
2 cloves garlic, mashed
¼ cup picante sauce
3 green onions, chopped
Salt
Corn chips

CHICKEN FAJITAS
Serves 6

Medium fresh shrimp, peeled and deveined, can be substituted for the chicken but should be marinated only for a few hours. I've also used sirloin grilled very rare and sliced very thin. A mixture of these three makes a festive menu for a large group.

Place chicken breasts in a glass dish. Rub with garlic and sprinkle with pepper. Add the lime juice and cover tightly. Refrigerate until ready to use.

Grill chicken over hot coals for 2 minutes per side; slice diagonally into strips. In a skillet cook onion in butter until limp but not yet translucent. Add green pepper and green chilies. Continue cooking until vegetables are crisp tender. Add sliced chicken and cook until heated through.

To serve, fill warmed tortillas with the chicken mixture, lettuce, salsa, guacamole, cheese, and sour cream.

6 boneless half breasts of chicken
2 cloves garlic, pressed
1 teaspoon freshly ground pepper
3 tablespoons lime juice
1 large onion, thinly sliced
1 tablespoon butter or margarine
1 large green pepper, sliced
2 large or 3 small fresh green chilies, sliced
12 flour tortillas
Lettuce
Salsa
Guacamole
Sour cream

BLACK REFRIED BEANS
Serves 6

Sort and wash beans. Place in a Dutch oven, cover with cold water and put on to cook. As soon as beans begin to soften (about 4 hours), cook onion in butter or margarine until soft and translucent. Add garlic and bacon and continue to cook slowly until the bacon is cooked but not crisp. Do not cook too fast or the garlic will burn and develop a bitter flavor. Add onion mixture to beans with cumin, oregano, pepper, and coriander. Allow to cook another 2 hours. Just before starting the fajitas, transfer the beans to a greased cast-iron skillet. Coarsely mash the beans. Stir in cheese, milk, salt, and vinegar. Simmer until ready to serve.

1½ cups black turtle beans (3 cups cooked)
1 large white onion, finely chopped
1 tablespoon butter or margarine
2 cloves garlic, minced
¼ pound bacon, cut into small pieces
1 teaspoon ground cumin
1 teaspoon dried Mexican oregano
1 teaspoon coarse ground pepper
½ teaspoon ground coriander
1 teaspoon salt
1 teaspoon cider vinegar
½ cup grated Monterey Jack cheese
¼ cup milk

CONFETTI COLESLAW

For dressing, in a jar combine oil, vinegar, salt, cumin, pepper, and garlic. Cover and shake well. In a large bowl combine cabbage, tomato, olives, onion, feta cheese, and cilantro. Add dressing, tossing to coat.

¼ cup vegetable oil
2 tablespoons tarragon or wine vinegar
¾ teaspoon salt
½ teaspoon ground cumin
Dash pepper
1 clove garlic, crushed
3 cups chopped red cabbage
1 medium tomato, chopped
⅓ cup sliced pimiento-stuffed olives
¼ cup chopped onion
¼ cup crumbled feta cheese
1 tablespoon snipped cilantro

1 medium cantaloupe, cut into
    chunks
2 bananas, sliced
1½ cups grapes, halved
2 medium avocadoes, peeled, pitted,
    and cut into chunks
½ cup flaked coconut, toasted
2 tablespoons lime juice
3 tablespoons honey
6 tablespoons rum

HONEY RUM FRUIT BOWL
Serves 6

In a bowl combine cantaloupe, bananas, grapes, avocadoes, and half of the coconut. Sprinkle with the lime juice and mix well. Drizzle with honey and rum. Stir to blend. Sprinkle top with remaining coconut.

½ cup water
1 cup sugar
1 cinnamon stick
1 lemon, unpeeled
1 orange, unpeeled
1 lime, unpeeled
Ice
1 quart dry red or white wine

SANGRIA

The syrup will keep in the refrigerator for at least one month.

In a saucepan stir together sugar, water, and cinammon stick. Boil over medium-high heat for five minutes; cool and remove the cinnamon stick. Roll the fruits on a hard surface to loosen the juice and cut into thick slices. Add to cooled syrup and chill for several hours.

Fill a glass pitcher with ice. Add the sliced fruit, half of the cinnamon syrup, and the wine. Stir the mixture thoroughly, mashing the fruit slightly. Serve in well-chilled tumblers, garnishing each glass with some of the sliced fruit. The remaining syrup can be added to the pitcher to make a second portion.

FLAN
Serves 8

Caramelize 1 cup sugar in a large skillet over medium heat, stirring constantly until sugar melts and browns (about 10 minutes). Pour into the bottoms of 8 buttered custard cups or one buttered custard mold. Immediately tip the cups back and forth to coat with the sugar. (Work fast, as the liquid will set rapidly.)

Beat egg yolks and eggs well; add milk, remaining sugar, and vanilla. Pour into cups or mold and sprinkle lightly with cinnamon. Set containers in a large baking pan and pour boiling water into the pan until it reaches halfway up the sides of the molds. Cover with foil and bake at 350 degrees for 1 hour. Remove foil and continue cooking another 10 minutes. Check custard by inserting a knife into the center. If it comes out clean the custard is ready. If using a single mold, you may need to bake the custard as much as 15 minutes longer.

To serve, place each cup in a pan of hot water for no more than a few seconds. This will melt the caramelized sugar so the flan slides out easily when turned onto a dessert plate. Serve warm or chilled.

1½ cups sugar
3 whole eggs
5 egg yolks
1 large can evaporated milk
1 can whole milk
2 teaspoons vanilla
Ground cinnamon

LAMBERT

8 breasts of chukar or 4 whole birds
⅛ cup flour
½ teaspoon salt
¼ teaspoon pepper
½ teaspoon paprika
½ bunch fresh parsley, chopped
1 cup onion, chopped
1 cup celery, sliced
1 cup mushrooms, sliced
1 jar pimientos, chopped
1 cup double-strength chicken
    bouillon
½ cup white wine
1 teaspoon thyme
1 teaspoon sage
¼ cup flour
2 tablespoons butter
1 cup heavy cream

NEVADA CHUKAR FEED

Hunting game birds is a favorite pastime in cowboy country. Duck, sage hens, doves, quail and other varieties are prized by ranch cooks. On that rare half-day of free time, ranch folk often pick up shotguns and head for the marsh or hayfield to bag a bird or two.

Chukar partridges native to India, were planted in Nevada about 40 years ago. They have flourished in the congenial habitat of dry hills and cheat grass. The chukar is a medium-sized bird with a slightly wild taste, not unlike chicken, and a light-colored meat.

We hunt chukar in early October, when frost has turned the leaves of the aspen gold and red, when the air is as crisp as a bite into a new apple. We like the chukar best cooked tender in a Dutch oven, with gravy to spoon over a mound of mashed potatoes.

BRAISED NEVADA CHUKAR
Serves 8

Each bird should be skinned, cut into three pieces—the breast and two legs. Wash the pieces well, being sure to remove any remaining shot. Combine the flour, salt, pepper and paprika. Dredge the chukar in the mixture and place the pieces in a greased Dutch oven or deep skillet. Brown each piece on all sides as well as possible. This may need to be done in batches as too many pieces at a time will prevent the coating from becoming brown and crisp. Once all the pieces have been browned, return all of them to the Dutch oven and cover with remaining ingredients except flour, butter and cream. Cook covered at 325 degrees for 1½ hours, or until tender. Remove the meat from the pan to an oven-proof platter. Return to the oven to keep it warm. Degrease the remaining stock if necessary. Make a paste of the flour and butter. Add to the drippings. Stir until thickened and flour is cooked, 3 to 5 minutes. Add cream and heat through. Spoon some of the gravy over the meat and sprinkle with fresh parsley. Spoon the mashed potatoes around the edge of the platter. Pass the remaining gravy.

Where chukar is unavailable, pheasant, quail or dove may be substituted.

LISTEN TO THE SUN GO DOWN
Leon Flick

Upon a warm September's eve,
the sun was dipping low.
I sat myself upon a rim,
from there to watch the show.

The shadows were their longest now,
as darkness soon would be.
I closed my eyes and listened
to the sounds I couldn't see.

The quail chatted nervously,
about to go to bed.
The hoot-owl screeched a different tune,
his whole night lay ahead.

The rock chuck whistled one last cry,
and from his warm rock he did slide.
The deer crept from the willows,
no longer there to hide.

The coyote howled from up on top,
before his nightly quest.
The wasps that had been buzzing
were now safe within their nest.

The magpie and the meadowlark
and rooster pheasant too,
All said, "see you in the morning,"
and off to roost they flew.

The bobcat didn't say much
as he tested out the air.
The porcupine wandered to the creek
to get a drink from there.

The nighthawks were coming about to life,
after hiding all day from the sun.
The muskrat and the beaver splashed,
Either working or having fun.

And I can promise you one thing,
you will smile instead of frown
If you'll close your eyes and open your ears
and listen to the sun go down.

10 medium potatoes, unpeeled
   and quartered
⅓ cup butter
½ cup milk or half & half
Salt
Pepper

MASHED POTATOES
Serves 8

Boil the potatoes until soft. Drain. Add butter and ½ the milk.
Using an electric mixer, whip the potatoes until light and fluffy. Add
milk as needed, being cautious not to make them too wet. Salt and
pepper to taste. Remove to serving bowl and top with a pat of butter
and a sprinkling of fresh parsley.

8 roma or Italian salad tomatoes
1 cup sherry
1 teaspoon dried oregano
¾ cup bread crumbs
¼ cup Parmesan cheese
½ cup butter
1 cup sour cream

BROILED SHERRIED TOMATOES
Serves 8

Cut the tomatoes in half and set them on a foil-covered baking sheet,
cut side up. If they won't stand straight, cut a small slice off the
bottom. Prick each half with a fork in several places and spoon 1
tablespoon of sherry over each tomato. Combine the bread crumbs
and the butter and top each tomato with 1 tablespoon of the
mixture. Place the tomatoes under the broiler and cook for 5 to 7
minutes, just until the crumbs have browned. Remove and quickly
top each with 1 tablespoon of sour cream.

1 small head butter lettuce
½ medium head romaine lettuce
1 bunch bibb lettuce
4 green onions, sliced
1 avocado, chopped
½ cup toasted walnuts
¼ cup freshly grated Parmesan
   cheese
⅓ cup white wine vinegar
¼ cup olive oil
½ cup walnut oil
Salt & pepper to taste

LEAF SALAD WITH WALNUT-OIL DRESSING
Serves 8-10

Mix the dressing ingredients well and set aside. Combine the salad
greens and set in the refrigerator until ready to serve. When you are
ready, pour a small amount of the dressing over the greens and toss.
Add the cheese and walnuts, more of the dressing and toss well.
Sprinkle with black pepper.

SIX-LAYER CARROT CAKE
Serves 12

Sift together the flour, salt, soda, cinnamon and sugar. Add the oil and the eggs and blend well. Add the carrots and stir. Pour into three 8-inch layer pans. Bake at 350 degrees for 35 to 40 minutes. When a toothpick inserted into the center comes out clean, the cake is done. Remove to a cooling rack for 10 minutes, run a knife around the edge and turn-out the layers. When they are fully cooled, prepare the filling, split the layers, fill and frost.

2 cups flour
1 teaspoon salt
1 teaspoon soda
2 teaspoons cinnamon
2 cups sugar
1½ cup oil
4 eggs, beaten
2 teaspoons vanilla
3 cups carrots, grated and cooked
1 cup walnuts, chopped and mixed
    with 1 tablespoon flour

Filling

Soften the cream cheese and margarine; beat together. Gradually add the sugar, mix well and blend in the vanilla. Split the first layer and place the top upside down on the cake plate, spread the layer with the filling and place the other half on top. Spread a portion of the frosting on the top, split the second layer and repeat. Finish with the third layer and frost the outside with the remaining filling. Excellent served with a vanilla coffee.

16 ounces cream cheese
¼ pound margarine
2 boxes powdered sugar, sifted
3 teaspoons vanilla

Katherine Field - 1935.

AFTER-HAYING BARBECUE

In hayfields across the West, grass stood tall and green under the sun. It was July, and the tedious work of walking miles of irrigation ditch had resulted in a good hay crop.

At first light, the hay crew headed to the fields. The work teams, heavy under harness, moved past one by one. The men spoke curt commands to their horses and sent messages with their hands through the long leather lines that lay along the horses' backs. Young boys in their first haying season rode out toward manhood behind the most trustworthy teams. By day's end, the hay had fallen in thick green ribbons and was raked and bucked and hoisted into bread-loaf stacks, a guarantee of feed for the stock through the winter.

Today the thump and whine of diesel-powered swathers and balers has replaced the jangling, creaky sounds of horse-drawn rigs. But the sense of celebration, of thanksgiving for a completed harvest, has not changed. This late-summer barbecue is designed to be prepared out-of-doors. Succulent beef and vegetables are cooked over an open fire and teamed with a signature salad from John Ascuaga's Nugget in Reno. Make-ahead apple pie and corn and cheese muffins round out a celebration meal that your co-workers and friends will remember!

¼ cup olive oil
2 cloves garlic, minced fine
1 teaspoon cracked pepper
6 pounds London Broil

LONDON BROIL WITH FRESH GARLIC AND CRACKED PEPPER
Serves 10

An hour before cooking, combine the oil, garlic, and pepper; spread evenly over both sides of the meat. Cover lightly and allow to remain at room temperature until ready to grill. Grill over medium coals for 6 minutes. Turn and grill to desired doneness. Cook 7 to 8 minutes more for medium-rare.

L.E. Wallis

THE HEAVYWEIGHT CHAMPION PIE-EATIN' COWBOY OF THE WEST
Paul Zarzyski

I just ate 50 pies—started off with coconut
macaroon, wedged my way through bar angel
chocolate, Marlborough, black walnut and sour cream
raisin to confetti-crusted crab apple—
still got room for dessert
and they can stick their J-E-L-L-O
where the cowpie don't shine, 'cause Sugar Plum,
I don't eat nothing made from horses' hooves!

So make it something "pie," something light
and fancy, like huckleberry fluffy chiffon, go
extra heavy on the hucks and fluff—beaten
egg whites folded in just so. Or let's shoot
for something in plaid, red and tan lattice-
topped raspberry, honeyed crust
flaky and blistered to a luster, wild
fruit oozing with a scoop of hard vanilla!

Or maybe I'll strap on a feedbag of something
a smidgen more timid: quivering
custard with its nutmeg-freckled fill
nervous in the shell. Come to think of it now,
blue ribbon mincemeat sounds a lot
more my cut: neck of venison, beef suet,
raisins, apples, citrus peel, currants—
all laced, Grammy-fashion, in blackstrap molasses!

No. Truth is, I'm craving shoofly or spiced rhubarb,
or sure hard to match peachy praline,
cinnamon winesap apple á la mode, walnut
crumb or chocolate pecan. OR,
whitecapped high above its fluted deep-dish crust,
a lemon angel meringue—not to mention
mandarin apricot, black bottom, banana cream,
burgundy berry or Bavarian nectarine ambrosia!

And how could you out-gun the Turkeyday
old reliables: sweet potato, its cousin
pumpkin, its sidekicks Dutch apple and cranberry
ice cream nut. Ah, harvest moon, that autumn
gourmet cheese supreme, or Jack Frost squash, or . . .
"my favorite," you ask? That's a tough one.
Just surprise me with something new, Sweetie
Pie—like tangerine boomerang gooseberry!

½ cup butter or margarine
7 russet potatoes, peeled and
  quartered
1 small garlic bulb, unpeeled and
  separated
½ teaspoon paprika
½ teaspoon salt
¼ teaspoon pepper

GARLICKY DUTCH OVEN BROWNS
Serves 10

Melt 2 tablespoons of the butter in the bottom of a Dutch oven. Add potato quarters and randomly drop in the unpeeled garlic cloves and remaining butter. Sprinkle with salt, paprika, and pepper. Clear a spot for the Dutch oven and surround it with the coals (to avoid burning potatoes). Cover and cook for 45 to 60 minutes or until tender. Move the Dutch oven directly onto the hot coals for 10 to 15 minutes or until the bottom of the potatoes brown. Or, place the covered Dutch oven in a 375 degree oven for 45 minutes; uncover and allow to crisp for 15 to 20 minutes before serving. Serve from the oven. Squeeze the cooked garlic over potatoes.

10 to 12 ears of fresh corn with
  husks and silk left on
Salted water
Melted butter or margarine
Salt
Pepper

GRILLED CORN ON THE COB

Prepare corn by washing the husks and removing any old or brown pieces. Using a piece of kitchen string, tie the husks of the corn to cover any exposed portions of the cob. Place the corn in enough salted water to cover and soak for 20 minutes; drain. Place cobs on grill for 15 minutes, rotating the cobs frequently. You should expect the husks to be slightly charred. The corn is done when the kernels show water when pierced with a fork or sharp knife. Remove from the grill, husk the corn and place on a platter with melted butter and salt and pepper to taste.

GRILLED VEGETABLE MEDLEY
Serves 10

For dressing, combine oil, vinegar, and garlic. Place eggplant, pattypan squash, peppers, zucchini, crookneck squash, and onion in a glass dish. Pour dressing over vegetables, tossing to coat. Let stand at room temperature for 2 hours. About 10 minutes before the meat is ready, begin placing the vegetables on the grill. Place the onions first and allow them to cook a minute or so before adding the zucchini, crookneck squash, and peppers. Follow 2 minutes later with the eggplant and pattypans. Grill for an additional 3 minutes; turn and grill another 3 or 4 minutes until the vegetables are tender. Remove to a warmed platter, sprinkle lightly with fresh balsamic vinegar and the basil. Season with salt and pepper.

¾ cup olive oil
½ cup Balsamic vinegar
2 cloves garlic, pressed
10 ½-inch thick slices eggplant
10 pattypan or scallop squash, cut in half
6 medium sweet red peppers, seeded and quartered
4 medium zucchini, sliced lengthwise ½ inch thick
5 small crookneck squash, halved lengthwise
1 or 2 red onions, sliced ½ inch thick
¼ cup chopped fresh basil
Salt
Freshly ground pepper

1½ cups olive oil

1¼ teaspoons Coleman's dry
mustard

1 teaspoon Worcestershire

½ teaspoon ground oregano

¼ teaspoon salt

¼ teaspoon seasoned salt

¼ teaspoon freshly ground pepper

¼ cup lemon juice

2 heads Romaine lettuce

¼ cup grated Parmesan cheese

¼ cup chopped green onions

¼ pound bacon, cooked crisp
and crumbled

1 cup croutons

2 coddled eggs (simmered about
10 minutes)

Grated Parmesan cheese

JOHN ASCUAGA'S CICERO SALAD
Serves 10

We happened across this salad recipe on the inside of a match book from John Ascuaga's Nugget Hotel and Casino, known throughout the western states for its food.

For dressing, stir together oil, mustard, Worcestershire sauce, oregano, salt, seasoned salt, and pepper. Add lemon juice, whisking till well combined.

In a bowl combine Romaine, croutons, Parmesan cheese, green onions, bacon, and eggs. Pour the dressing over the Romaine mixture, tossing to coat. Sprinkle with a bit more Parmesan cheese before serving.

Note: Homemade croutons make this salad especially good. Day-old bread can be used. Cut it into ¼-inch squares. Toss with ½ cup melted butter, ¼ cup snipped parsley, ½ teaspoon dried thyme, and ½ teaspoon dried oregano. Bake at 300 degrees for 20 minutes or till bread is light brown and crisp.

¾ cup butter or margarine

1 cup sugar

4 eggs

1 8-ounce can corn

1 4-ounce can chopped green
chilies

1 cup buttermilk

1 cup sour cream

½ cup shredded sharp
cheddar cheese

1 cup flour

1 cup yellow corn meal

4 teaspoons baking powder

½ teaspoon salt

CHEESY CORN MUFFINS
Makes 24

In a bowl beat butter with an electric mixer till softened. Add sugar and beat till light and fluffy. Add eggs, one at a time, beating well after each. Add corn, chilies, milk, sour cream, and cheese. Stir together flour, cornmeal, baking powder, and salt; add to corn mixture. Beat till well combined. Pour into a greased 13x9-inch baking pan. Place in a preheated 350-degree oven and immediately reduce the heat to 300 degrees. Bake for 1 hour.

BOURBON APPLE PIE
Serves 8

Several hours before preparing the pie, place the raisins in a small bowl and cover with the bourbon.

Prepare pastry. Roll out half the dough and line the bottom of a 10-inch deep-dish pie plate.

In a large bowl, combine the sugar, flour, cinnamon, salt, and nutmeg. Add the apples, walnuts, and undrained raisins and bourbon. Mix well and pour into prepared pie crust. Dot the top with butter and cover with top crust.

Vent and place in lower third of oven. Bake at 425 degrees for 50 to 60 minutes or till crust is golden brown. Serve warm or cooled with a scoop of vanilla ice cream.

½ cup raisins
¼ cup bourbon (use a rye whiskey, not a smooth or blended variety)
Pastry for a 2-crust pie
¾ **cup sugar**
2 tablespoons flour
1 teaspoon ground cinnamon
¼ **teaspoon salt**
⅛ **teaspoon ground nutmeg**
7 cups peeled and sliced Granny Smith apples
½ **cup toasted walnut pieces tossed with 1 teaspoon flour**
3 tablespoons butter or margarine
Vanilla ice cream

MENU

HAM BAKED IN BEER

SWEET MUSTARD SAUCE

RAE'S RANCH BEANS

GRANDMA MAC'S REFRIGERATOR ROLLS

FRESH FRUIT SALAD

WATERCRESS AND SLICED TOMATOES

MARIONBERRY COBBLER

1 8- to 10-pound bone-in ham
12 ounces beer
Sweet Mustard Sauce

BRANDING PICNIC

Near noon on a clear day. Inside the pole corrals cattle circle nervously as a man on horseback moves through them. His right hand rests against his leather-covered thigh, the loop of a lariat folded into his palm. A white-faced calf darts away from the rest, the man's arm swings out, and the loop snakes out and snares the calf by its hind feet. The man dallies his rope around the saddle horn, and his horse moves against the taut line, pulling the bawling calf toward the branding fire and the waiting ground crew.

As the hot iron is applied and the smoke swirls, a pickup bumps up to the corral. From its bed come bowls, crocks, baskets, boxes, Dutch ovens, coolers. The tailgate of the pickup folds down to form a table loaded with pots of beans cooked with bacon and onion, piles of fat yeast rolls, thick slices of roast beef or ham, bowls of salads, pies and cakes and crocks of lemonade. Cowboys and ground crew slap dust from their hats and shirts as they line up to fill tin plates and cups for the noon meal.

HAM BAKED IN BEER

Place the ham in a large Dutch oven or roasting pan and pour beer over the top. Bake at 350 degrees for approximately 15 minutes per pound. Baste with additional beer and pan juices while ham bakes. Serve with mustard sauce. Or, make a gravy by skimming the fat from the juices. Add a little flour and milk. Cook and stir till thickened and bubbly. Season with salt and pepper.

THE BRANDING LUNCH
Wally McRae

It's not just the hustle, the fun, or the bustle,
The squalling and bawling and smoke;
The sweat speckled brow, the charge of a cow;
The din or the grin from a joke.
It's not just the glow of the coals burning low
From a crackling wood fire, I've a hunch,
That makes a man warm and his senses just swarm,
In contemplation of lunch.
It defies understanding how a meal so outstanding
Should have such an inglorious name.
For lunch at a branding should share equal standing
With meals of gastronomic fame.

Caviar or escargot I'd gladly forego
For a slab of rare roast beef.
Some beans piled high will make us sigh
For our hunger's beyond belief.
Some cole slaw? Aye! Some hot apple pie!
Black coffee! Say, I've got a hunch
If you've dined at The Ritz (or more high-class outfits),
It can't compare with a good branding lunch.

Katherine Field –35.

1 cup light cream
½ cup sugar
1 heaping teaspoon dry mustard
2 egg yolks, beaten
¼ cup cider vinegar
Salt

SWEET MUSTARD SAUCE

In the top of a double boiler stir together cream, sugar, and mustard. Blend in beaten yolks and slowly add vinegar. Cook and stir over simmering water until thick. Serve with ham.

---

3 cups dry pinto beans
12 cups water
7 slices bacon
1 medium onion, chopped
1 8-ounce can tomato sauce
Salt
Pepper

RAE'S RANCH BEANS
Serves 6

Leftover beans can be made into soup. Add a clove of mashed garlic, a can of whole tomatoes, sliced cabbage, and grated carrots.

Choose a kettle large enough to hold beans and water. (Remember the beans will swell.) Sort and wash the beans. Place in kettle and cover with water; soak overnight. (If you wish, you can pour off the water and replace with fresh in the morning.) Cover the bean pot and place it on the stove. Bring to a boil; reduce heat. Simmer on low heat until beans are tender. The time will vary by altitude and freshness of the beans, but cooking will take approximately 2 to 3 hours.

When the beans are almost tender, chop the bacon and cook over slow heat until cooked through but not crisp. Add the onions and cook until tender. Add onion mixture and tomato sauce to beans. Add additional water if needed. When beans are fully cooked, salt and pepper to taste.

---

1 package dry yeast
½ cup warm water
1 cup boiling water
¼ cup butter or margarine
2 tablespoons sugar
1¼ teaspoons salt
1 egg, beaten
3 cups flour, sifted
1 egg white combined with
    1 tablespoon water

GRANDMA MAC'S REFRIGERATOR ROLLS

Dissolve the yeast in the warm water. Combine the boiling water, butter, sugar, and salt; cool. Beat in egg till well combined. Add the yeast and flour; beat well. Cover the bowl with a light cloth and place in the refrigerator for 6 to 8 hours. Remove to a lightly floured board. Shape dough into rolls, using additional flour as needed to keep them from sticking. Place in a glass baking dish and let rise for 1 hour. Bake at 425 degrees for 15 minutes. Remove and brush with egg white mixture. Return to oven for 5 minutes more or until golden brown.

½ cup vegetable oil
½ cup tarragon flavored
   white wine vinegar
¼ cup honey
¼ cup orange juice concentrate
1 teaspoon salt
1 teaspoon poppy seeds
½ teaspoon ground ginger
⅛ teaspoon dry mustard
2 bananas, sliced
1 cup cantaloupe or honeydew
   melon balls
1 apple, chopped
1 cup seedless grapes, halved
1 orange, separated into sections
¾ cup strawberries
¼ cup slivered almonds (optional)

FRESH-FRUIT SALAD
Serves 6

For dressing stir together oil, vinegar, honey, orange juice concentrate, salt, poppy seeds, ginger, and mustard. Combine dressing ingredients and set aside. In a bowl combine bananas, melon, grapes, orange, and strawberries. Pour dressing over fruit, tossing to coat. Sprinkle with almonds, if desired. Store any leftover dressing in the refrigerator.

½ cup olive oil
¼ cup red wine vinegar
1 teaspoon Dijon mustard
½ teaspoon sugar
½ teaspoon salt
Pepper
3 medium red tomatoes
2 bunches watercress, washed and
   stems removed
3 slices bacon, cooked crisp and
   crumbled
3 heaping teaspoons snipped fresh
   basil

WATERCRESS AND SLICED TOMATOES

For dressing, in a jar combine oil, vinegar, mustard, and salt. Season with pepper. Cover and shake till well combined. Let stand at room temperature. Remove tomatoes from refrigerator about 15 minutes before serving. Slice and drizzle lightly with some of the dressing. At serving time, toss the watercress with bacon and half of the basil. Drizzle lightly with dressing and place on a serving plate. Top with the tomatoes and remaining dressing, slightly overlapping the tomatoes. Sprinkle with the remaining basil.

MARIONBERRY COBBLER
Serves 12

You can successfully substitute blueberries, raspberries, or sliced peaches for the Marion blackberries.

In a saucepan stir together water and sugar. Bring to a boil. Cook and stir for 4 to 5 minutes or until the sugar is dissolved. Set aside to cool slightly. Stir together flour, sugar, baking powder, and salt. Cut in the shortening till mixture resembles coarse crumbs. Add the milk to make a soft dough. Spread the dough evenly on the bottom of a greased 13x9-inch baking pan. Place the berries evenly over the top and pour the sugar mixture over fruit. Bake in a preheated 375-degree oven for 45 minutes. Serve hot or at room temperature with cream or ice cream.

1 cup water
½ cup sugar
2 cups unbleached flour
1 cup sugar
2 tablespoons baking powder
½ teaspoon salt
⅔ cup shortening
1 cup milk
5 to 6 cups fresh or frozen Marion blackberries
Heavy cream or vanilla ice cream

KatherineField. 33

4 slices bacon

4 brook trout, about ½ pound each, cleaned and scaled

¼ cup flour, seasoned with salt and pepper

CAMPFIRE TROUT

The golden light of late afternoon sifts through the trees and plays on the surface of the stream rippling around your feet. You can feel its cold pressure against your waders. Suddenly the line in your left hand goes taut, and the end of your pole bends down toward the water: a strike! You bring the line in, your reel clicking, and a flash of silver cuts through the water in front of you. You play the fish closer, use your net, and bring out of the water a rainbow trout, just frying-pan size.

Fresh trout cooked in the open are a western specialty. This trout menu is simple enough to prepare completely outdoors, although you might want to bake the cake ahead and carry it with you. Liquid ingredients for the pan biscuits can be premeasured and added to the premixed dry ingredients when your fire is hot. If your trip is too long to carry perishables, you can replace the spinach and dandelion green salad with one made of canned green beans, chopped hard-boiled eggs, vinegar and oil, salt and pepper.

This meal is especially memorable when followed by a colorful sunset and a few cowboy songs under the stars.

PANFRIED TROUT WITH BACON
Serves 4

In a skillet fry bacon till crisp; drain on paper towels, reserving bacon grease (use cooked bacon in salad). Dredge the fish in the flour mixture. Add fish to hot bacon grease and cook for 2 to 3 minutes or until the fish is brown. Turn and cook for 4 to 5 minutes more or till fish is tender. Remove the fish to a warm plate and serve.

GIVE US A SONG, IAN TYSON
Wallace McRae

Write me a tune, Ian Tyson,
With a beat sort of easy and slow,
That will flow down each valley and canyon
From Alberta to Old Mexico.
Make it sound like the wind in the pine trees
Or the plains muffled deep in the snow.
Yes, please, write me a tune, Ian Tyson,
Like an old one the cowboys all know.

Write down some words, Ian Tyson,
Words that put a sad tear in my eye.
Words that speak of the unspoken yearning
That I have for the old days gone by.
Tell again of our shame, or our glory,
With a shout, or perhaps with a sigh.
Won't you write down some words, Ian Tyson,
Of the West, 'neath a big open sky?

Sing me your song, Ian Tyson,
Would you sing your song only for me?
Let the ripples of music transport me
Like the waves carry ships on the sea.
Make me fight, or just languidly listen.
Sing of strife, or of sweet harmony.
But please sing me your song, Ian Tyson,
Sing it softly and easy and free.

Teach us your song, Ian Tyson,
So the cowboys can all sing along.
And forgive when we stumble and mumble,
Or we get the verses all wrong.
It's your fate to be placed as the hero
Of a bowlegged buckaroo throng.
So we'll borrow your song, Ian Tyson,
And then call it our own cowboy song.

They'll steal your song, Ian Tyson,
Steal the song that the cowboys love well,
And they'll change both the beat and the lyrics,
And they'll merchandise it with hard sell.
Let the Nashvillains ride plastic ponies
Round and round on their fake carousel.
Yet your song will remain on the ranches
Of the West, where the true cowboys dwell.

Thanks for your song, Ian Tyson,
For the ballad that crept from your pen.
Out here into our hearts in the heartland,
To the home of the true saddlemen.
For we're weary tonight of the strident,
Of the tedious rock regimen.
So, please sing one more time, Ian Tyson,
Your song. Yes, sing it again.

2 tablespoons bacon grease or
    shortening
4 medium potatoes, peeled and
    sliced
1 small onion, sliced
1 to 2 cloves garlic, finely chopped
4 tablespoons chopped parsley
    (optional)
4 slices bacon, cooked crisp and
    crumbled (optional)

BUCKAROO POTATOES
Serves 4

Put grease in the bottom of a Dutch oven and heat it until the grease begins to smoke. Place the potatoes, onions and garlic in the oven. Cook and stir until the potatoes begin to brown. Put a lid on the Dutch oven and lower the heat. Gently simmer the potatoes until they are soft. Just before serving, return the pan to medium high until the potatoes are crisp. If desired, add parsley and bacon.

2 tablespoons red wine vinegar
2 tablespoons bacon drippings
2 tablespoons vegetable oil
1 clove garlic, pressed
Salt
Pepper
1 handful fresh spinach
1 handful fresh dandelion greens
1 handful mixed greens such as
    arugula and radicchio
1 small red onion, sliced
4 mushrooms, sliced
1 egg, hard-boiled and sliced

DANDELION-SPINACH SALAD WITH BACON DRESSING
Serves 4

For dressing, stir together vinegar, bacon drippings, oil, and garlic. Season with salt and pepper. In a large bowl combine spinach, dandelion greens, mixed greens, onion, mushroom, and egg. Pour dressing over spinach mixture, tossing gently to coat.

½ cup milk
2 tablespoons vegetable oil
1 tablespoon vinegar
½ teaspoon onion powder
1 cup unbleached flour
½ cup cornmeal
1 tablespoon baking powder
1 tablespoon sugar
½ teaspoon salt
½ teaspoon soda
2 tablespoons butter or margarine

PAN BISCUITS
Makes 18 biscuits

In a measuring cup, combine the milk, oil, vinegar, and onion powder. In a mixing bowl stir together flour, cornmeal, baking powder, sugar, salt, and baking soda. Stir in the milk mixture with a fork. Form the dough into a ball and turn out onto a lightly floured surface. Knead it about 10 times. Shape the dough into 18 smooth balls about 1½ inches in diameter; flatten with the palm of your hand to a thickness of about ½ inch. In a skillet, melt butter or margarine over medium-low heat; add the biscuits. Cook over the coals until lightly browned on both sides and cooked through, approximately 15 minutes.

RHUBARB CAKE

In a bowl beat ½ cup butter with an electric mixer till softened. Add brown sugar and beat till fluffy. Beat in egg and vanilla. Stir together flour and baking soda. Add to butter mixture alternately with the milk. (Be sure you begin with the dry ingredients and end with the dry ingredients.) Fold in the sour cream just until it is blended. Do not over-mix. Stir in the rhubarb and walnuts. Spread the batter in a greased and floured 8x8-inch pan. Stir together sugar cinnamon. Cut in 1 tablespoon butter till coarse crumbs. Stir in nuts. Sprinkle over rhubarb mixture. Bake at 350 degrees for 40 to 50 minutes.

½ cup butter or margarine
1½ cups packed brown sugar
2 eggs
1 teaspoon vanilla
2 cups flour
1 teaspoon baking soda
½ cup milk
½ cup sour cream
1½ cups chopped raw rhubarb
½ cup chopped walnuts
¼ cup white sugar
1 teaspoon cinnamon
1 tablespoon butter or margarine

ROUNDUP
CELEBRATION

The shipping of cattle marks the end of a cycle to the cowboy. He has seen the calves born in early spring, branded them in summer, gathered them in fall, fed them through a cold winter, watched them grow stout and fat in summer pasture. Now he rounds them up, cuts out the market steers and trails them to the holding pens to be loaded onto railroad cars or cattle trucks and shipped east. There is a quiet sense of celebration in shipping: the work is done, and the check in the pocket runs the outfit for another year. Our roundup celebration features the bounty of harvest season.

MENU

STUFFED PORK LOIN ROAST

WILD RICE AND PINE NUT CASSEROLE

ACORN SQUASH ROUNDS

LOO'S WINED APPLES

SOURDOUGH BREAD

THREE-LEAF SALAD WITH RED GRAPES

STEAMED GREEN BEANS

PECAN PIE

ELDERBERRY PIE

PUMPKIN CHEESECAKE WITH BRANDY SAUCE

1 6-rib center-cut pork loin roast
4 cups seasoned bread crumbs
1 pound bulk pork sausage
1 bunch spinach, steamed, drained, and chopped, or one 10-ounce package frozen chopped spinach, cooked and drained
1 medium onion, finely chopped
¼ cup grated Parmesan cheese
3 eggs, lightly beaten
1 clove garlic, pressed
¼ teaspoon pepper
Butter or margarine
2¼ cups chicken broth
½ teaspoon dried basil
3 tablespoons flour
Salt
Pepper

STUFFED PORK LOIN ROAST
Serves 6

Several days before the celebration, order the roast from the butcher. Ask him to crack the back and shin bones for easy serving.

For stuffing, stir together bread crumbs, sausage, spinach, onion, cheese, eggs, and pepper. Set aside. Make 5 deep slashes between the ribs on the meaty side of the roast. Pack ¼ to ⅓ cup stuffing into each slash. Place the remaining stuffing in a small casserole. Top with butter and bake at 325 degrees for 30 minutes. Wrap the roast in a single layer of cheese cloth and tie loosely. Roast uncovered on the bottom rack of a 325 degree oven for 2 ½ to 3 hours or until meat reaches 160 degrees. Turn off the oven, remove the roast to a serving platter and return it to the oven. (Continued p. 88)

When They've Finished Shipping Cattle in the Fall

Bruce Kiskaddon (excerpt)

Though you're not exactly blue,
Yet you don't feel like you do
In the winter, or the long hot summer days.
For your feelin's and the weather,
Seem to sort of go together,
And you're quiet in the dreamy autumn haze.
When the last big steer is goaded
Down the chute, and safely loaded;
And the summer crew has ceased to hit the ball;
When a feller starts a-draggin'
To the home ranch with the wagon—
When they've finished shippin' cattle in the fall.

Only two men left a standin'
On the job for winter brandin',
And your pardner he's a loafin' at your side.
With a bran new saddle creakin',
Neither one of you is speakin',
And you feel it's goin' to be a silent ride.
But you savvy one another,
For you know him like a brother,
He is friendly but he's quiet, that is all;
He is thinkin' while he's draggin'
To the home ranch with the wagon—
When they've finished shippin' cattle in the fall.

And the saddle hosses stringin'
At an easy walk a swingin'
In behind the old chuckwagon movin' slow.
They are weary, gaunt and jaded
With the mud and brush they've waded,
And they settled down to business long ago.
Not a hoss is feelin' sporty,
Not a hoss is actin' snorty;
In the spring the brutes was full of buck and bawl;
But they're gentle, when they're draggin'
To the home ranch with the wagon,
When they've finished shippin' cattle in the fall. . . .

Katherine Field - 35

For the gravy, skim the fat from the roasting pan and add ¼ cup of the chicken broth. Scrape the pan, getting as much of the drippings as possible. Stir in basil and flour. Cook and stir until thickened and bubbly. Gradually add the remaining 2 cups of broth. Season with salt and pepper. Slice the meat and top with a small amount of the gravy. Pass the remaining gravy separately.

¼ cup chopped parsley
½ teaspoon dried thyme
1 bay leaf
1½ cups chicken broth
1 cup wild rice
½ cup long grain rice
8 ounces fresh mushrooms, sliced
½ teaspoon fresh ground pepper
¾ cup pine nuts, toasted
⅓ cup chopped onion
½ cup butter or margarine
3 tablespoons flour
1 cup milk
½ cup seasoned bread crumbs
2 tablespoons melted butter or
   margarine

WILD RICE AND PINE NUT CASSEROLE
Serves 6

Make a bouquet garni by placing parsley, thyme, and bay leaf in cheesecloth; tie ends. In a saucepan combine the chicken broth, wild rice, long grain rice, and bouquet garni bag. Bring to boiling; reduce heat. Cover and simmer for ½ hour. Meanwhile, cook onion in ½ cup butter till tender. Add mushrooms and pepper and cook until the mushrooms are limp. Stir together milk and flour. When the wild rice is tender, stir in onion mixture, pinenuts, and milk mixture. Transfer to a large casserole dish. Bake at 325 degrees for 30 minutes. Remove the dish from the oven. (This recipe can be prepared to this point early in the day and placed in the refrigerator. Remove from refrigerator 1 hour before serving. Remove bouquet garni bag.)

Stir together bread crumbs and 2 tablespoons butter or margarine. Sprinkle over wild rice mixture. Bake, uncovered, for 30 minutes more.

2 acorn squash
½ cup packed brown sugar
½ cup butter or margarine

ACORN SQUASH ROUNDS
Serves 6

Cut the unpeeled squash into slices approximately ¾ inch thick. Using a sharp knife, remove the seeds and membranes from the center. Place the slices on a foil-covered baking sheet and sprinkle with half of the brown sugar. Dot with half of the butter. Bake at 400 degrees for 15 minutes. Using a spatula, carefully turn the slices and spread with remaining sugar and butter. Return to the oven for 10 minutes more or until tender.

LOO'S WINED APPLES
Serves 6

Place the lemon peel in cheesecloth; tie ends to make a bag. Cut the apples into thick slices. In a skillet cook apple slices in butter or margarine for 3 minutes. Sprinkle with the sugar. Stir in water, wine, and lemon juice. Add lemon peel. Bring to boiling; reduce heat. Cover and simmer until the apple slices are tender but still whole.

Grated peel from 1 lemon
2 pounds apples, washed, peeled and cored
2 tablespoons butter or margarine
½ cup sugar
½ cup water
½ cup dry white wine
1 tablespoon lemon juice

SOURDOUGH BREAD

The night before, in a non-reactive bowl, use a wooden spoon to stir together starter, 1 cup water, salt, and sugar. Stir in 2 cups flour. Cover with a cloth and let stand at room temperature overnight.

Dissolve yeast in 1½ cups warm water. After 10 minutes, add the starter mixture and the 5 to 6 cups flour, 1 cup at a time, stirring until you have a very stiff dough. Knead on a lightly floured surface about 7 minutes or until smooth. Place in a well buttered bowl. Cover and let rise in a warm place for 1½ to 2 hours or until double.

Punch down dough; return to the bowl. Let rise again for 1 hour. Turn out and divide in half. Shape into 2 round loaves and place on a baking sheet sprinkled with corn meal. Slash the top with a sharp knife in 2 or 3 places. Let rise 1 hour. Preheat oven to 400 degrees and place a shallow pan of boiling water on the lowest rack. Place bread on the rack above the water and bake for 35 to 40 minutes or until the bread sounds hollow when rapped with your knuckles.

Sponge
1 cup Sourdough Starter (see pp.12-14)
1 cup warm water
2 teaspoons salt
1 teaspoon sugar
2 cups flour

Bread
1 package dry yeast
1½ cups warm water
5 to 6 cups flour
½ teaspoon baking soda

THREE-LEAF SALAD WITH RED GRAPES
Serves 8

For dressing, in a jar combine oil, vinegar, salt, pepper, and garlic. Cover and shake till well combined. In a large bowl combine lettuces, shrimp, grapes, sprouts, almonds, and mushrooms. Pour dressing over lettuce mixture, tossing to coat.

⅔ cup olive oil
½ cup red wine vinegar
½ teaspoon salt
¼ teaspoon freshly ground pepper
2 cloves garlic, pressed
1 small head butter lettuce
1 small head green leaf lettuce
½ small head red leaf lettuce
1 pound medium shrimp, cooked, peeled, and deveined
1 cup red seedless grapes, halved
½ cup bean sprouts
¼ cup sliced almonds
8 mushrooms, sliced

1½ pounds green beans
1 red pepper
Green onions
½ cup butter or margarine, melted
¼ cup grated Parmesan cheese
Salt
Pepper

STEAMED GREEN BEANS

Wash and trim the beans. Slice the pepper into long strips. Gather approximately 10 beans of similar size and one slice of red pepper into a bunch. Tie them together using strips of green onion tops. Repeat this procedure until all the beans are "packaged." Place them in a steamer basket and place over boiling water. Steam the beans approximately 20 minutes or until tender but not soft. Place cooked bean packages on a serving platter and drizzle with the butter. Sprinkle with Parmesan cheese. Season with salt and pepper.

Pastry for a 1-crust deep dish pie
3 eggs
1 cup sugar
1 cup light corn syrup
1 teaspoon vanilla
2 cups chopped pecans
¼ cup butter or margarine,
   melted and cooled

PECAN PIE
Serves 8

Place the pastry in a 10-inch deep dish pie plate. Flute the edges. In a bowl beat eggs with an electric mixer on high for 3 minutes. Add the sugar, corn syrup, and vanilla. Beat for 2 minutes more or until thick and caramel colored. Stir in the pecans and melted butter or margarine. Pour into the unbaked pie shell. Bake at 350 degrees for 1 hour or till a knife inserted near the center comes out clean.

Pastry for a 2-crust pie
4 cups elderberries
1 cup sugar
3½ tablespoons tapioca
1½ tablespoons lemon juice
3 tablespoons butter or margarine

ELDERBERRY PIE

Place half of the pastry into a 9-inch pie plate. Stir together berries, sugar, tapioca, and lemon juice. Pour into the pie crust. Dot with butter and top with the remaining crust. Vent the crust in several places. Bake at 450 degrees for 15 minutes; reduce the heat to 350 degrees and bake for 30 minutes or until the juice is bubbling and the crust is golden brown.

GRANDMA'S NEVER-FAIL PIE CRUST

This recipe came to us from both poet Sunny Martin of Ely, NV, and rancher Claudia Riordan of Jiggs, NV.

3 cups flour
1 scant teaspoon cream of tartar
1 teaspoon sugar
1 teaspoon salt
1¼ cups shortening
5 or 6 tablespoons cold water
1 egg
1 teaspoon vinegar

In a bowl stir together flour, cream of tartar, sugar, and salt. Using a pastry blender, cut in the shortening until the mixture resembles peas and crumbles easily. In a small bowl or cup stir together cold water, egg, and vinegar. Pour over the flour mixture, stirring lightly with a fork until all the flour is dampened. Knead lightly several times; then roll out enough dough, on a floured board, for the bottom crust.

If you are making a shell to be filled later, be sure to heat the pie pan before adding the crust. Heating the pie pan will allow the dough to relax so it does not shrink. The dough will become shiny, but that does not affect its tenderness or flakiness. After placing and trimming the crust, prick well around the sides and bottom and turn the extra dough under to double the edges for fluting. Bake at 450 degrees for 12 to 15 minutes. The dough for a single-crust pie should be somewhat drier than for a double-crust pie.

If you are making a double crust pie, roll out the top crust and with a sharp knife, make a small design in the dough for steam to vent. Fill bottom crust with filling; add top crust and trim with scissors about ½ inch smaller than the bottom crust. Roll bottom crust over top crust and flute.

6 graham crackers, crushed
½ cup finely chopped pecans
¼ cup packed brown sugar
½ cup butter or margarine, melted

3 8-ounce packages cream cheese,
     softened
¼ cup butter or margarine
¾ cup packed brown sugar
½ cup granulated sugar
5 large eggs
1 16-ounce can solid-pack pumpkin
1 teaspoon ground cinnamon
½ teaspoon ground ginger
1 teaspoon vanilla
1 cup sour cream

½ cup packed brown sugar
1 tablespoon cornstarch
¾ cup cold water
2 tablespoons brandy
1 tablespoon butter or margarine

PUMPKIN CHEESECAKE WITH BRANDY SAUCE

Serves 10

Crust

Combine cracker crumbs, nuts, and sugar. Stir in melted butter.
Press mixture into the bottom of a 9-inch springform pan. Set aside.

Filling

In a mixing bowl beat cream cheese and butter or margarine till well
combined. Add sugars and beat till light and fluffy. Add the eggs,
one at a time, beating well after each addition. Beat in pumpkin,
cinnamon, ginger and vanilla. Mix well. On lowest speed add the
sour cream and beat until just mixed through. Pour batter over crust
and bake in a 325-degree oven for 45 to 55 minutes. Cake is ready
when the center no longer appears to move. Remove cake from
oven and cool to room temperature. Place in refrigerator overnight.

Brandy Sauce

In a saucepan, combine the sugar and cornstarch. Stir in cold water.
Cook and stir over medium-high heat until thick and boiling.
Remove and cool slightly. Stir in brandy. Add butter, beating well
after each addition. Let stand at room temperature till cool. Pour 2
tablespoons over each cheesecake slice before serving. Pass
remaining sauce.

Katherine Field -85

INDEX

COWBOY BOOKS AVAILABLE FROM GIBBS SMITH, PUBLISHER

Cowboy poems, songs, and recipes filled with the humor and warmth of the ranching West may be ordered by phone or mail.

COWBOY POETRY

A Gathering

This collection of poems, both humorous and serious, was chosen from among 10,000 gathered from cowboy reciters, ranch poets, and from a library of over 200 published works of cowboy verse. A third of the poems are classics that have lived in the minds and hearts of cowboys and ranchers of the West for several decades. Two-thirds of the poems in this volume are new, created within the last few years.

192 pp.; 4 x 6½; illustrations; jacketed paperback, $9.95.

NEW COWBOY POETRY

A Contemporary Gathering

These recent works are from America's best cowboy and cowgirl poets, most of whom are regular participants in the cowboy poetry gatherings held from state to state and the grandaddy gathering held each January in Elko, Nevada. Included in this anthology are some of the best-known poets, such as Waddie Mitchell and Wally McRae. Most of the poets use traditional rhyme scheme and meter; a few push the bounds of tradition and introduce the reader to free verse, cowboy style. But no matter how these poems are structured, the poets breathe reality into the myth of the buckaroos and ranching life.

176 pp.; 4 x 6½; jacketed paperback, $9.95.

COWBOY CURMUDGEON AND OTHER POEMS

Wallace McRae

Wally McRae is a classic among today's cowboy poets. He has appeared on "The Tonight Show" and recites his poems regularly on a syndicated television program, "The West." In 1990 he became the first cowboy poet to be granted a National Heritage Award from the NEA in Washington, D.C.

This book collects more than 100 of his most popular poems, including classics such as "Reincarnation " and "Give Us a Song, Ian Tyson," along with forty new poems published here for the first time.

144 pp.; 6 x 9; illustrated; paperback, $9.95.

OLD-TIME COWBOY SONGS

The Bunkhouse Orchestra

More than fifty well-loved songs of pioneers, plainsmen, and cowpunchers are collected in this book, which includes melody lines, guitar chords, and complete lyrics to each song. The accompanying tape contains ten of the songs, plus familiar cowboy dance tunes of the day, performed in renditions certain to bring a smile to any listener. Most of these tunes were composed between 1880 and 1930.

Book: 96 pp., 4¼ x 6¼; illustrated; paper. Cassette tape: 45 minutes. Packaged together in an attractive full-color box. $15.95.
